GW00385229

UNBELIEVING HUSBANDS

the neglected harvest

UNBELIEVING HUSBANDS

the neglected harvest

Ann M. Velia

UNBELIEVING HUSBANDS
the neglected harvest

© 2008 Ann M. Velia
All rights reserved
Printed in the United States of America

Unless otherwise indicated, all scriptures are from the King James Version. Emphasis through italicization has been added by the author.

Cover design and page layout by David Siglin of A&E Media

ISBN 978-1-932307-86-3

Published by the Ambassador Group

Ambassador International
427 Wade Hampton Blvd.
Greenville, SC 29609
USA
www.emeraldhouse.com

and

Ambassador Publications Ltd.
Providence House
Ardenlee Street
Belfast BT6 8QJ
Northern Ireland
www.ambassador-productions.com

The colophon is a trademark of Ambassador

Dedication

To Jim — the hero of my story

Acknowledgements

Much prayer, encouragement, and technical support helped bring this book to completion. I am especially grateful to:

- my husband Jim, for assistance at every level
- Jewell Johnson, my writing mentor and friend
- Pastor Felix O. Gonzales, who hosted the pilot study from which this book evolved
- the women in that pilot group: Char, Diane, JoAnn, Maria, and (in memoriam) Barbara
- five special couples whom I love very much: Ed and Donna, Charlie and Carol, John and Shirley, Henry and Betty, and James and Lucy
- My Emmaus reunion group
- the Treasure Seekers bible study group
- our friends, the "Friday Nighters" -- with special thanks to my computer guru, David Amaral
- the experts at Ambassador Intl.: Dr. Samuel Lowry, Timothy Lowry and David Siglin

Table of Contents

CHAPTER 1

Spiritually-Divided Marriages

The Dismal Multiplication of Neglect

ONCE UPON A TIME — LOTTIE'S STORY, PART I

Bud, a free-spirited older man, breezed into Lottie's south Texas hometown and captured her heart. They dated only a few months before Bud took a job as a crewman in an oil field several hundred miles away, and — long before the days of e-mail and text messaging — their romance distilled into telephone calls, letters and an occasional surprise visit when Bud drove his sporty car across the distance that separated them.

Handsome, charming, always sharply dressed for their dates, Bud sprinkled stars in Lottie's eyes. And he loved Lottie enough to pursue his courtship across the miles.

Bud prized Lottie's reputation as "a good Christian girl." He came from a churchgoing family, although a different denomination from Lottie's. He was a bit more worldly than Lottie's previous beaus, but he willingly went to Sunday morning services with her on his weekend visits.

Within the year, they were married in her family's church.

Immediately afterward, Bud moved Lottie to the oil-drilling camp, quite a change from her hometown. The popular newlyweds were quickly absorbed into the close-knit society, where weekends were devoted to parties and group activities.

Lottie, far from her own family, snuggled into the embrace of those new friends.

Churchgoing got crowded out of the picture.

❧

The Lord Jesus Christ said in John 4:35, "...Lift up your eyes, and look on the fields; for they are white already to harvest."

As the twentieth century drew to a close, the Church looked particularly long and hard at fields of people who hadn't yet heard the gospel — the "good news" of God's provision for salvation through faith in Christ.

Expert planning and missionary zeal were evident as new churches were planted at home and overseas. Radio and television stations beamed the gospel beyond national borders. City-wide evangelism crusades took place throughout America. People signed pledges to pray daily for their neighborhoods. Interdenominational groups rallied concentrated prayer for specific populations, notably for people along the Mexican-American border and for the mostly-Muslim nations in the eastern hemisphere.

But one field was — and is — *overlooked* by the church: the field of unbelieving men married to Christian women.

When the church *does* "look on" that field, its glance may range from sympathetic but basically helpless, to impatient, to indignant — even to hostile. (It seems that every layman knows 2 Corinthians 6:14: "Be ye not unequally yoked together with unbelievers....")

To be fair, our fellow Christians probably haven't had opportunity to get to know our husbands, so it's hard for them to make sensible comments or constructive suggestions about our situations.

And few churches offer any formal help to the frustrated wives in their congregations. Even pastors may subtly condemn them for "a problem of their own making" or inadvertently turn them away from church.

THE CHURCH'S NEGLECT STEMS FROM ITS DIFFERENT FOCUS

The local church is geared, first, to serve people who enter its doors, with discipleship training for believers and evangelistic preaching for spiritual seekers.

Unbelieving husbands are usually diligent to avoid church attendance.

And while "go and tell" evangelism is the strong suit of the church, husbands scattered throughout town in their faith-divided homes are too elusive a group to fit into a church's outreach programs.

GIVE THE CHURCH CREDIT FOR THE JOB IT DOES

The believing community properly pools its funds and prayer support for bigger mission fields.

It's a serious enterprise to prepare workers to do the going and the telling. Experts in strategy, culture, linguistics, and logistics train missionaries to represent the rest of us in fulfilling the Great Commission "unto the uttermost part of the earth."

Missionaries within our country, too, are oriented to the needs of distinctive groups of people, so they can work effectively in areas like crosscultural evangelism in ethnic neighborhoods, jail ministry, vacation bible school and other child-evangelism work, and nursing home visitation.

Even those citywide revivals include training sessions for workers who will follow up with new converts.

The church has a good handle on equipping people for "go and tell" evangelism.

NOT 'GO AND TELL' BUT 'STAY AND SHOW'

The neglected field calls for different methods, however. The scant biblical instructions for reaching spiritually-dormant husbands is directed to their wives.

The tactic: "stay and show" rather than "go and tell" is not very good sermon material for a minister to preach to the general congregation.

Most pastors can quote the relevant scriptures, or at least point them out to the wives, but often that is as far as "equipping for ministry" goes.

And the sometimes-desperate question, "What can I do to help my husband believe?" is likely to be answered with the pat summation: "All you can do is pray, let your light shine, and leave him in God's hands." This isn't wrong advice, by the way. It's just short on detail and rationale.

In some 35 years of church attendance, I have never found a class which provided specific preparation, or even a support group for women like me — married to a man who does not share my faith.

My friend Jodie concurs. She visited a number of churches after she committed her life to Christ six years ago. She laments, "I never saw a church that catered to our circumstances. Our situation has never, ever, ever been addressed by any church I've gone to."

She lives an active church life, but she notes, "Married women whose husbands don't attend are an 'off-brand' at church. We feel awkward in groups geared for couples, but we can't join the singles' meetings, either."

And while churches are attentive to strengthening marriages and families, the classes they offer are typically designed for husband and wife participation — as are sweetheart banquets, family camps and couples' retreats.

THE WIFE MAY BEGIN TO NEGLECT HER MARITAL VOWS

Most of us promised, before God and witnesses, to love, to honor, and — if we pledged very traditional vows — possibly to do something else which we'll discuss in a later chapter. Suffice it for now to consider how faith differences take a toll on every facet of the marriage:

- people who were once mutual friends suffer by comparison with the wife's new friends, whose lives revolve around church activities. She invests less time, and less interest, in her old social life
- financial support for the church is likely to meet strong opposition from an uncommitted husband
- children are confused by divided beliefs between their parents, and may feel they have to "take sides"
- differences in moral values are ammunition for accusation and argument
- emotional ties with church friends weaken or may even replace a woman's emotional connection with her spouse
- physical intimacy falls away with the weakening of emotional closeness, and misunderstood bible teachings about marital roles may trouble both partners
- "love and honor" may be less and less frequently demonstrated by both sides of a divided home, and
- resentment against her husband builds as the wife blames him for her marginal place in church life.

THE WIFE NEGLECTS HER DEVOTIONAL LIFE

Many forces conspire to hinder a woman's desire to grow in her faith. Her husband may be offended by her books, her music, her retreat into prayer. She is reluctant to be overheard by her husband when she is discussing "church stuff" with a Christian friend on the telephone.

She may feel she has to go elsewhere — to church — to practice her faith freely.

Church is certainly an easier place to "let her light shine" than at home. And, face it, the hubbub of activity in committees and women's groups, fundraisers, making the church festive with seasonal decorations and planning fellowship events is exciting.

Women generally are very welcome to participate in local outreach to those nursing homes or the community soup kitchen. Women flock to interdenominational events like National Day of Prayer services.

A woman whose home life is spiritually sterile likes to engage with people who unabashedly love God, and who appreciate her contributions to their programs.

The catch is, she is likely to spend inordinate time on activities which rob her of personal time with the Lord.

And just because she has a whole new realm of interests doesn't excuse her from the ordinary duties of life, which still consume as much time as ever. Her schedule overflows.

THE WIFE NEGLECTS 'KEEPING AT HOME'

I'm sure by now you are checking the copyright date on this book. But, yes, "keeping at home" is one of the "good things" us older women are told to teach the younger women (see Titus 2:3-5).

An older neighbor once told me, "There are only two times a man wants his wife to be at home — when he's there, and when he's not."

Technology enables us to serve as a check-in center whether we're at home or elsewhere. But it is comforting to a husband or child to know that the woman of the house will be around at predictable times. It should be gratifying to us to realize how valuable we are as the heart of the home.

But read "keeping at home" as "housekeeping," and I'm sure you're getting ready to fling this book out the window. This is the 21st century, and everybody shares the chores!

Fair enough, particularly when both spouses hold jobs.

Let's render that archaic term as "homekeeping," however, and see what pictures of comfort, security and peace come to mind. Providing those qualities requires a focus on homelife which is diluted when church life becomes paramount in a wife's affections.

ALL THIS NEGLECT ULTIMATELY AFFECTS THE HAPLESS HUSBAND

One day he was minding his own business, and suddenly everything in his marriage began to change — for the worse, from his perspective.

No wonder he's resistant to celebrating his wife's newfound joy. His belief hasn't changed. Nor has anything else, from his side.

He still likes to schedule activities on weekends, rather than losing his family to a church schedule — and a Sunday morning service cuts the weekend right in half.

His pagan friends are still his friends, and he defends their lifestyle as much as he protects his own.

His financial plan doesn't include supporting religious programs.

What did *he* do to deserve all this disruption in his wife and his home?

SO — WHAT CAN WE DO?

First, we cut some slack to pastors and laymen for ways they have failed or disappointed us.

Next, accept that our challenge differs from other ways of sharing the gospel.

Then we study those scant references the pastor recited to see what they actually say.

We "look on our field" analytically and consider how to apply the teachings in our unique marriages.

We search for other advice that the God who hasn't overlooked us reveals in His word.

We discover, I'm afraid, that the instructions can't be delegated back to the pastor, our Sunday school teacher, our best friends, or the prayer line. We're the ones who need to do the things that can make a difference.

TWO THINGS TO KEEP IN MIND:

When you decide to concentrate on household ministry, someone will point out to you I Corinthians 7:16: "For what knowest thou, O wife, whether thou shalt save thy husband?"

It's an important point. There are no guarantees. I haven't seen fulfillment yet in my marriage.

But neither are other missionaries guaranteed success. For all of us, preparing the way of the Lord is a work of faith.

Second, in the worst case, a husband may end the marriage to his Christian wife.

Scripture advises (I Corinthians 7:15), "But if the unbelieving depart, let him depart. A brother or a sister is not under bondage in such cases, but God has called us to peace."

A husband's departure naturally aborts your mission commitment — and it can happen even when it seems you are making progress in drawing him toward Christ.

This is the time to claim your pastor's advice and support. He is, sadly, well-acquainted with separation and divorce.

I believe that if your marriage ends, God has another way to reach your husband — and He has an alternate plan for you.

But let's see how we can lessen the chances that your husband will leave, and increase the chances that your faith in Christ will become irresistible.

LOTTIE'S STORY, PART 2

Bud and Lottie lived in a house trailer Bud had built, nicely-finished and equipped with clever features of his own design in each small room.

And that sporty car was a cut above anyone else's.

Bud was exciting, he was fun, Lottie was happy.

She missed her parents and siblings, but Bud was her family now. And the family was about to grow. She was pregnant.

AUTHOR'S NOTE:

You'll find exercises at the end of each chapter to guide you in personalizing its principles.

Space is provided for you to write in this book, and I hope you will do the bible studies within these pages.

However, when an exercise calls for personal information about you or your husband, I recommend using a separate notebook, such as a prayer journal or a looseleaf binder. You may want to review and update some of the information as circumstances change.

You may also want to share this book with a friend, or let your pastor examine it with a view to starting a class for unequally-yoked wives.

Writing your answers in a separate place will keep them confidential between you and the Lord.

P.S. Exercises are things that produce the best results when they are repeated!

EXERCISE 1

REALITY CHECK: HOW DID I END UP IN A SPIRITUALLY-UNEQUAL MARRIAGE?

Be honest!

- I assumed my husband-to-be was a Christian
- I deceived myself about my husband's relationship with Christ
- My husband deceived me about his faith. (In what way?)
- I wanted to believe he was a godly man, and I overlooked contrary evidence.
- I pieced together enough good points to "sell him" as Mr. Right to people who expressed doubts about him.

or

- I had no spiritual standards, no faith of my own. His spiritual state was of no concern.
- I came to Christ, or renewed my commitment to Him, after I married.
- I've told my husband why I am now a follower of Christ. (His reaction?)

or

- We both genuinely practiced our faith when we married, but he fell away. (Do you know why?)

Go over your answers in prayer, unburdening your heart to God. Keep giving Him your disappointments and guilt until you have fully released them.

Be assured that God loves you AND your husband, and He wants to be glorified in your marriage.

EXERCISE 2

THE ONGOING WORK OF FORGIVENESS

1. In prayer, forgive every Christian leader or layman who has hurt or discouraged you by:
   - their indifference
   - thoughtless remarks
   - subtle (or outright!) condemnation of your unequal marriage
   - or by dismissing your cries for help with pat answers.

Be as specific as possible as you recall and declare "forgiven" over each offense.

Keep repeating this exercise until you release all resentment against your sisters and brothers in Christ.

Now — thank God for the church's "go and tell" outreach. Pray that some of their evangelism targets will overlap into the neglected field of unbelieving husbands.

2. In prayer, forgive your husband for his coldness to your faith, and for every hurtful remark he has made. Keep on forgiving him.

3. Pray for understanding of how your husband is hurt by the spiritual division in your marriage.

Thank God that you have been reconciled to Him, and that He is now present in your home, abiding in you!

EXERCISE 3

'LOOK ON THE FIELD' - DISCOVERY PROJECT

What hinders your husband's ability or willingness to believe or to commit his life to Christ? (You may not know all the answers, but you probably have clues. Be alert for more.)

- his past experiences with church people
- wounds from his past
- his relationships with his father, his mother, or siblings
- marital wounds
- intellectual pride
- competitiveness with you over your job success, popularity, etc.
- an independent spirit
- discomfort with your superior knowledge and experience as a Christian
- fear that you will continue to be the "spiritual leader" in your marriage
- your complaints about church and other Christians
- your exuberant admiration for a pastor or Christian teacher
- other

Pray for God's forgiveness of any way you have given your husband a poor impression of Christ's followers, or the fear that he no longer measures up in your eyes.

Ask God to give your husband insight into his hindering influences, and enable him to rise above their power.

EXERCISE 4

MAXIMIZE YOUR ASSETS: THINGS YOU LOVE ABOUT YOUR HUSBAND

Philippians 4:8 says, "...whatsoever things are true, whatsoever things are honest, whatsoever things are just, whatsoever things are pure, whatsoever things are lovely, whatsoever things are of good report: if there be any virtue, and if there be any praise, think on these things."

Answer the following questions:

What attracted you to your husband when you first met him? Do you still enjoy that attribute in him?

If not, why not?

What are your husband's good points

- physically
- intellectually
- emotionally
- morally
- concerning his work
- in his treatment of you
- in his fatherly activities?

What are your favorite memories of shared activities with him?

Re-read your answers to these questions regularly, adding new information as it occurs to you. — and keep this positive mental portrait in your heart.

EXERCISE 5

WHAT DOES YOUR HUSBAND LOVE ABOUT YOU?

Proverbs 18:22 says: Whoso findeth a wife findeth a good thing, and obtaineth favour of the Lord.

If your husband were to read this verse, would he believe it?

What was the basis of his attraction to you?

Is that attribute still part of "the package"?

If not, why not?

How do you rate with him

- physically
- intellectually
- emotionally
- morally
- as a loving wife
- as a mother to his children?

If applicable, are you both happy with you being employed outside the home?

- if not, why not?

Do you think your husband is proud of you?

Why, or why not?

Re-read this page regularly, rejoicing over the positives, and praying about any negatives.

CHAPTER 2

Household Missionary: A Motivating Model

Neglected "Jerusalem"

LOTTIE'S STORY: BACK IN CHURCH

A year after their wedding, Bud and Lottie's firstborn child arrived, a daughter they named Harriet.

Both Lottie and Bud's religious denominations practiced infant baptism. They agreed it was an important rite.

Lottie called a church in the city nearest the drilling camp and introduced herself over the telephone. She made arrangements for Harriet's baptism the following Sunday.

That morning, Bud overslept. Lottie roused him several times, and he finally struggled out of bed.

He seemed to have had a lead transfusion. He moved in slow motion, but finally got dressed and ready to go.

Thanks to that speedy car, they made it to the church just before the service started.

Bud stood shoulder to shoulder with Lottie during the baptism. After service, the pastor and several church members greeted the young family and urged them to come back the following Sunday.

Bud suddenly recovered his normal speed and hustled Lottie and the baby into their car.

Two years later, Bud found an opportunity to go into business for himself, which involved a move into town.

When Lottie and Bud baptized their second baby, a boy, the pastor said, "We wish you would make yourselves at home in our church. Your little girl is nearly old enough for our toddler's Sunday school class."

Lottie felt a hunger to attend church, and a conviction that she should take Harriet to Sunday school. Bud didn't object. "Just so you don't expect me to go with you," he said.

So Lottie would leave him to sleep late on Sunday mornings while she quietly fed and dressed the children and drove to church.

People crowded around her to admire the children. "How come you don't bring your husband with you?" one old man asked every week, as though he suspected Lottie kept him chained in the backyard so he wouldn't follow them to church.

"He's still in bed," Lottie explained, slightly amused at his persistent question. "He works awfully hard during the week and needs a little extra sleep on weekends."

HOUSEHOLD MISSIONARY: A MOTIVATING MODEL

Just before the Lord Jesus ascended into heaven, he told his disciples to wait in Jerusalem until they received power through the Holy Ghost. Afterward, he said, "...ye shall be witnesses unto me both in Jerusalem, and in all Judea, and in Samaria, and unto the uttermost part of the earth" (Acts 1:8).

Jerusalem was *where they were*. They were told to give their report in the city they started from, then throughout their nation, into the neighboring country, and into all the world.

"Jerusalem" is where *you* are when you receive your call to make Christ known to others.

If you are married to a man who is indifferent to Christ, your home is a worthy and important place to begin. In fact, you are the most likely disciple who can influence your husband to believe, through the intimate, day-to-day evidence of Christ's life-giving, life-changing power at work in you.

Home is also the most difficult place to live a consistent, godly life. That makes it an ideal place for intense spiritual growth to develop!

WE'RE IN THE GAME, WITHOUT THE NAME

There is an odd resistance by people outside our situation to call the wife a "missionary" to him. The constraint against a wife preaching at her husband may be part of the problem. After all, Romans 10:14 asks, "How shall they hear without a preacher?"

"Faith cometh by hearing" is another truth that points to the power of speaking God's word to ignite faith.

So if a wife is cautioned against "preaching" or "spouting bible verses," how can she be a minister of the gospel to him?

But what role is assigned to us with the usual advice: "Pray, let your light shine, and leave him in God's hands"? Isn't that recognition of our playing a part in influencing him for Christ (without preaching)?

The idea seems to be that calling us "missionaries" would put a heavy burden on us, making us feel that we are failing every day that our husbands continue to resist Christ.

The alternative, we are often told, is to "find ways to cope with the challenges of living with an unbeliever."

In other words, tend to your own needs. Leave it up to the Lord to tend to your husband's need for salvation.

Well...if He hadn't given us those tantalizing verses connecting our behavior and our attitudes to "winning him," we could be satisfied with that easier advice.

But we are "household missionaries" by divine appointment if the unbelieving husband *chooses to stay with his believing wife*.

I Corinthians 7:13-14 says, "...if he be pleased to dwell with her, let her not leave him. For the unbelieving husband is sanctified by the wife...else were your children unclean. But now they are holy."

The husband is not *saved*; that requires the commitment of his will. But he is *set apart* because of his bond to you.

Talk about a head start! Missionaries to foreign tribes don't have that advantage!

NOT 'GO AND TELL,' BUT 'STAY AND SHOW'

So, missionary wife, how do we compare with those the church is pleased to call "missionaries"?

Our work takes place in familiar territory, and yet we face similar challenges with evangelists on a foreign field:

- loneliness
- separation from full access to the church (foreign missionaries also have to miss a lot of sweetheart banquets)
- learning to use a different "language" (the silent rather than the spoken gospel)
- bridging differences in culture and values that may be more and more evident as we grow in virtue and our husband may not.

Our strategies differ from those of "go and tell" missionaries. Our commission is to "stay and show." We just stay right where we are — in our "Jerusalem."

We don't need passports, we don't have to take nasty shots, we probably don't have to check the bedclothes for tarantulas before we turn in at night.

But other missionaries receive training and support from a sending organization.

- They have a recognized office in ministry.
- They interact with the church through conventions, visits to sponsoring congregations, and publications (and their photographs on bookmarks or refrigerator magnets to remind you to pray for them).
- Other missionaries have time to confirm their call to service, and, actually, the choice to accept or refuse the call.
- They form relationships with churches that support them with prayer and finances, and they report progress and changing conditions to their sponsors.
- They have time to put their affairs in order before they report to the mission site.
- They often have a commissioning ceremony to send them on their way.
- They get furloughs!

Household missionaries are on the job every day, all day, for an indeterminate time that could last for years.

While we already have an established relationship with our "mission field" — that head start! — the emotional dynamics are intensified for us. We already love our "field" — but we may have to re-learn to love him as the burdens of spiritual division take their toll.

We're on our own financially, but we're in good company! Acts 18:2-3 reveals that Paul, Priscilla and Aquila, all busy evangelists, supported themselves by tentmaking rather than by raising church pledges. And you will soon see another connection: they were tentmakers — we are home builders.

Paul and his colleagues did perhaps receive more prayer support and moral support than we will. Our fellow churchgoers are likely to criticize a household missionary for, say, a decision to go bowling with her husband rather than to attend a special event at church and insist that he come with her.

So, what do home missionaries do?

OUR PARTICULAR STRATEGIES:

We prepare the way of the Lord by

- removing hindrances
- getting wisdom and understanding

and

- building our homes.

Our "Jerusalem" is the home we share with our husband. It is just as worthy a place to serve Christ as is the church office or a Sunday school classroom — perhaps more so, because our work in the home is work only we can do. Church jobs can be filled by other people.

The overall task is to prepare the way of the Lord into our husbands' hearts.

John the Baptist, a "front man" for the Lord Jesus, quoted the prophet Isaiah in his preaching: "...Prepare ye the way of the Lord, make his paths straight. Every valley shall be filled, and every mountain and hill shall be brought low; and the crooked shall be made straight, and the rough ways shall be made smooth."

Picture the kind of work that would have been done to prepare a suitable roadway. You've seen highway construction projects, where the terrain is drastically changed — hillsides dynamited down, truckloads of rock dumped into low spots, or bridges built over a deep chasm or river — lots of preparatory work to remove obstacles to a smooth path.

REMOVING HINDRANCES: PREPARATION FOR HOUSEHOLD MINISTRY.

There are at least three types of hindrances that need to be cleared.

First, there are problems between ourselves and God that dim the light we want to shine before our husbands.

A particular problem for unequally-yoked wives is self-condemnation. We know that Christ's cross has covered all our sins — and yet, remaining in an unequal marriage seems like we are continuing in sin. After all, a repentant thief stops stealing, doesn't he?

And, whether we took such a drastic step as to deliberately marry outside God's will, or if we came to Christ late in life, there are doubtless other sins that took place in both our premarital and our pre-Christian or backslidden lives.

So, there's a lurking suspicion that we are only partially forgiven and can't expect anything better than "to lie in the beds we have made."

Please memorize this verse: "And the woman which hath an husband that believeth not, and if he be pleased to dwell with her, let her not leave him" (I Corinthians 7:13).

If your husband is willing to stay, God is willing to work. He honors the marriage, so we mustn't disparage it.

As for our being overachieving wrongdoers in the past, Jesus Himself said of a woman who was well-known as a sinner (see Luke 7:37-50), "Her sins, which are many, are forgiven; for she loved much..."

Where sin abounds, His grace *much more* abounds. You are *fully* forgiven.

A second problem for us is that we feel like second-class members of the church — unable to serve, or to give, or even to attend services as freely as the "equally-yoked" or the unattached.

It's like our lives are unsatisfactory on two fronts.

Missionary wife, you are the *first-class representative of God* in your home, His personal ambassador. Revel in that!

We do have the same issues to guard against, or to put off, as every other Christian:

- We will need to deal with our own rebellion, that contrary nature that continually opposes what we know is right.
- We need to keep check on our resentments, which insidiously turn into bitterness, and poison the other people in our lives.
- We need to guard against our lack of love — the indifference that we allow to affect us when we get tired of trying.
- We need to realize the harm our complaints can do to discourage other people — especially our husbands.
- We need to defeat our ingratitude with thanksgiving.

Wrong attitudes mar the image of Christ in us.

Then there are hindrances between ourselves and our husbands that we will need to address through

- seeking and granting forgiveness
- pursuing peace
- and by laying down our lives for him when our interests conflict.

By now, you're probably sensing that our strategies mostly have to do with letting God change *us*. Bingo! That's the major way to influence him.

We can, however, tackle some of the issues that hinder our husbands' relationship with God, through discovery projects — "looking on the field" — for insights that can make our prayers more effectual.

AFTER WE CLEAR, WE BUILD

In a sense, we "plant a church" when we prepare a Christ-honoring home characterized by peace, order and love. It needs also to be a husband-honoring home, founded on respect for him.

Then, while Christ is preparing a place for us in His Father's house, we concurrently prepare a place for Him in our hearts, through disciplined personal devotions. When we abide in Christ, and He abides in us, holy work takes place in our character.

WE CLARIFY OUR GOAL FOR OUR HUSBANDS

Behavior change in our husbands is likely to happen when we repair old damage and lessen the threat our husbands feel from our devotion to Christ. But our objective must always be to bring them *to Christ* — not to our set of standards or preferences, and not necessarily to *the church we have chosen.*

WE ALSO ACCEPT SCRIPTURAL GOALS FOR OURSELVES

The Apostle Peter describes qualities which will please both God and our husbands: purity, reverence, and a gentle and quiet spirit.

Homelife is the perfect beauty salon, because the necessary treatments to attain these enhancements are submission, sacrifice and servanthood — even ickier-sounding than permanent-wave solution and mud packs — but much more effective and long-lasting.

WE 'LET PATIENCE HAVE HER PERFECT WORK'

James 1:3-4 says, "Knowing this, that the trying of your faith worketh patience. But let patience have her perfect work, that ye may be perfect and entire, wanting nothing."

There are two aspects to patience: to wait, and to persevere.

It will often seem like our lives have been put on hold while we wait for our husbands to join us in faith. But God uses waiting time to teach us things we can't learn from — well, from reading a book.

Persevering is the active form of patience. It's like being on a diet — faithfully do the right things and you'll begin to see gratifying results.

God is at work all the while, through and even apart from our obedience. We may miss what He is doing, however, because we tire of waiting rather than capturing the wisdom we could gain. James 1: 5 continues: "If any of you lack wisdom, let him ask of God, that giveth to all men liberally, and upbraideth not, and it shall be given him."

CONSIDER THE REWARDS

Saint Paul wrote that Jesus endured the cross for the joy that was set before him.

Looking ahead to what our sacrifice — our laying down of our lives — can produce is also our motivation to endure the process.

The hope in most of our hearts is that our one-on-one ministry to our husbands will eventually result in our going two-by-two into the service of the church.

Without a doubt, we will bring our marital relationship to a stronger love and harmony than before spiritual division troubled us.

Our husbands and children will have good reason to "arise up and call us blessed," as did the family of the Virtuous Woman of Proverbs 31.

We will develop character qualities prized by both men and God.

We will deepen our relationship with Christ.

We will lead a more coherent, satisfying life.

We will "find rest for our souls" by streamlining our activities.

So — shazam! You're a household missionary!

LOTTIE'S STORY: BUD'S LAST CHURCH VISIT

Bud put in his reluctant appearance for baptisms numbers three — another boy and four — another girl. With baby number four, Bud's foot-dragging caused them to arrive at the church in mid-service.

"Well, here you are," the pastor said, from the pulpit. "We called for you a few minutes ago and figured you'd changed your minds. But come on up here — we'll do it now."

Lottie was so embarrassed she sat through the rest of the service with her head bowed.

The pastor hurried toward her and Bud as soon as he gave the benediction. "I'm glad you came today," he said, smiling his forgiveness. "Now come stand at the door with me so folks can see your pretty new daughter."

Bud stuck a cigarette in his mouth and flicked his lighter as they started toward the exit.

"Let's not smoke here in the sanctuary," the pastor said. His smile tightened, and so did his hand on Bud's elbow.

Lottie was the one in a hurry this time. "We need to get on home," she said.

EXERCISE 1

CREATE A MISSION STATEMENT

A mission statement is a good piece of equipment for a household missionary to have. Here's an example:

My mission is to manifest Christ in my home through being a "suitable helper" to my husband — willing, loving and cooperative — and to strengthen the bonds of oneness both in my marriage and in my life in Christ.

Now write a statement appropriate for your personal mission field.

Keep a copy of your mission statement inside your planner, and look at it when you make out your daily schedule.

EXERCISE 2

GETTING DOWN TO BUSINESS: REMOVING HINDRANCES BETWEEN OURSELVES AND GOD

Consider the following sins and spend a few minutes confessing each one that applies to you:

- for marrying in rebellion to scripture or to parental or pastoral counsel
- for other sins of rebellion
- for letting your love for God grow cold
- for neglecting your vows to love and honor your husband
- for walking outside the light in your marriage
- for murmuring and complaining
- for backbiting your Christian brethren
- for lack of diligent study and application of God's word
- for prayerlessness
- other

Read Psalm 51:1-13 as a prayer to God.

EXERCISE 3

LOOK IN THE BIBLE: SPECIFIC SCRIPTURES ADDRESSED TO WIVES WITH UNBELIEVING HUSBANDS

Write out the following scriptures from your favorite study bible. Consider that these words were provided specifically to answer your question, "What can I do to help him believe?"

I Peter 3:1-6:

I Corinthians 7:10-17:

Read the verses daily, with a reverent expectation that you will grow in understanding and application of God's powerful word.

EXERCISE 4

LOOK IN THE BIBLE:
SPECIFIC SCRIPTURES ADDRESSED TO ALL WIVES

Write out the following verses from your favorite study bible. Circle the words that also appeared in the scriptures addressed to wives of unbelievers.

Ephesians 5:22-24

Colossians 3:18

I Timothy 2:9-15

Titus 2:3-5

Now copy:
Proverbs 31:10-11

Proverbs 31:23

Proverbs 31:26-31

Underline references to the husband of this virtuous woman.

Now read the entirety of Proverbs 31:10-31 and meditate on how the virtuous woman's life impacted her husband.

EXERCISE 5

WHAT ARE YOUR HOPES FOR YOUR HUSBAND?

- To have him fill that empty spot next to me in the church pew.
- To have him respect my faith and my church involvement.
- To have him support me in teaching my children Christian values
- To have him know Christ as Savior, even if he has a deathbed conversion.
- To have him know Christ as both Savior and Lord of his life.
- To see him fulfill God's purposes for him in His Kingdom
- For God to restore the years he lost while he lived in unbelief, with time for him to store up treasures in heaven.
- Other

Do you have a "missionary's heart"? Assured of your own salvation, how much are you willing to sacrifice, or even to suffer, to see your husband come to belief in Christ?

Pray about this.

CHAPTER 3

Who You Are, Where You Are, Whose You Are

The Neglected Houseguest

LOTTIE'S STORY: ALL THOSE CHILDREN, AND NO DADDY?

Lottie continued to get herself and the children ready for Sunday school and church every week.

Women who recognized the effort it cost Lottie to bring her brood to church clucked, "All those children and no daddy?" Lottie realized they meant it as a tribute to her singlehanded feat, but it began to rankle.

The women's Sunday school class Lottie attended while the children went to their age-grouped classes was a welcome retreat every week. And she could hardly feel lonely in church service when she was surrounded by her own four children.

Then Lottie got a telephone call informing her that her younger daughter's Sunday school teacher was moving out of town. Would Lottie consider taking her place? She gladly agreed, excited to be able to contribute to the work of the church.

But there was a downside. "I felt like teaching little ones was expected of me because I had so many children in Sunday school," she said. "Before long, I felt like I didn't even know how to talk to an adult."

While other churchgoers — couples — stood in clusters to chat before worship service, Lottie gathered her youngsters from their various Sunday school classes and the family huddled together in a pew near the back door.

Until one morning when Lottie and her kids showed up at the sanctuary door and headed for their usual place.

An usher blocked their path. "We have a new policy," he told Lottie. "We're going to seat all the people with small children in the balcony so they won't distract the other worshippers."

"My children are well-behaved," Lottie protested. "We always sit right here at the back of the church, and my kids have never disturbed anybody." She looked at the narrow stairway where the usher herded her family.

"We can't very well make an exception just for you," he said.

Lottie trudged up the stairs to the ranks of balcony seats, her offspring following behind.

The reason for the policy became clear. Other parents held whiny tots, other children played with noisy toys, and Lottie could barely hear the sermon over the hubbub.

Three weeks later, Lottie made a self-punishing decision. She would continue with Sunday school, because her kids needed it. Forget the church service, where they were only conditionally welcome.

But after nursing her hurt feelings for several more days, she called the Sunday school superintendent to resign her teaching post. She would drop her kids off for Sunday school, and pick them up afterwards. As for her, she was calling it quits.

THE SAINT AT YOUR HOME ADDRESS

In his New Testament letters, Paul addressed "the saints in Christ Jesus at Ephesus... Philippi... Colosse," declaring their eternal position IN Christ, and their earthly location AT the named city.

You, missionary wife, are the saint IN Christ Jesus AT your home address.

Our *position* and *location* were established by commitments we made.

We abide <u>in</u> Christ because we committed our lives to Him.

We abide <u>with</u> a husband legally and morally because we made a commitment to him.

These two transactions produced phenomenal effects:

Through commitment to Christ we became ONE BODY with Him and with other believers.

Through commitment to our husbands, we became ONE FLESH with him.

Paul talks about both of these unions in Epesians 5:28-33: "So ought men to love their wives as their own *bodies*. He that loveth his wife loveth himself. For no man ever yet hated *his own flesh*; but nourisheth and cherisheth it, even as the Lord the church; For we are members of *his body*, of his flesh, and of his bones. For this cause shall a man leave his father and mother, and shall be joined unto his wife, and they two shall be *one flesh.* This is a great mystery: but I speak concerning Christ and the church. Nevertheless let every one of you in particular so love his wife even as himself: and the wife see that she reverence her husband" (emphasis added).

Marriage is the most binding human relationship, the one God exalts as a picture of the bond between Christ and His Church. Even though we are spiritually bound together, there are practical responsibilities for us.

Our work concerns two spiritual "buildings": the one in our hearts where Christ abides, and the emotional environment we share with our husbands.

THE LIVING PRESENCE OF CHRIST

Jesus taught that the integrity of a house depends on a strong foundation. "Therefore whosoever heareth these sayings of mine, and doeth them, I will liken him unto a *wise man*, which built his house upon a rock: and the rain descended, and the floods came, and the winds blew, and beat upon that house; and it fell not: for it was founded upon a rock. And every one that heareth these sayings of mine, and doeth them not, shall be likened unto a *foolish man*, which built his house upon the sand: And the rain descended, and the floods came, and the winds blew, and beat upon that house; and it fell: and great was the fall of it" (Matthew 7:24-27 - emphasis added).

This scripture, of course, refers to building a solid faith in Christ by hearing and doing what He has taught.

Does this seem like a huge diversion from "how to encourage a husband toward belief?"

Actually, the two great loves of our lives — love for our husbands and love for our God — are intimately connected. Let's see how.

My heart:
Christ's home within me
built on
TRUST IN HIS WORK,
OBEDIENCE TO HIS WORD
and
DELIGHT IN ALL THAT HE IS

Part of Paul's prayer for the Ephesians was "That (our Father) would grant you, according to the riches of his glory, to be strengthened with might by his Spirit *in the inner man*; That Christ may dwell i*n your hearts* by faith; that ye, being rooted and grounded in love, may be able to comprehend with all saints what is the breadth, and length, and depth, and height; and to know the love of Christ, which passeth knowledge, that ye might be filled with all the fulness of God" (Ephesians 3:16-19 - emphasis added).

Think of it — Christ living within *your* heart, the Holy Spirit strengthening *your* "inner man," rooting and grounding *you* in love, filling *you* with all the fullness of God.

Wouldn't that make you the live-in, living Presence of Christ in your home?

Earlier in this chapter we looked at the two places we occupy: *position* and *location*. We are IN Christ AT the space we take up on this planet.

Andrew Murray says, "The whole Christian life depends on the clear consciousness of our position in Christ" (*Abide in Christ*, Barbour and Company, Inc. Uhrichsville OH 44683).

In Christ we are accepted.

In Christ we are beloved by the Father.

In Christ we are held by the Everlasting Arms.

Now let's contrast *position* and *condition*. We are IN Christ because of His work of salvation coupled with our faith in what He has done on our behalf. Our *position* is steady, secure.

Our *condition* varies, however, depending upon how much we allow Christ to abide in us. Some days we are full of faith. Some days we are full of doubts.

In some situations we can resist the pull of peer pressure or wrong appetites. At other times, we feel as feeble against wrongdoing or wrong thinking as any unbeliever.

Sometimes we *feel* like a Christian — sometimes we don't. Sometimes we *act* like a Christian, sometimes we don't. Sometimes we *look* like a Christian — sometimes we don't.

HINDRANCES TO HIS ABIDING FULLNESS

We are always <u>in Christ</u>, and He always desires to fill His rightful place <u>in us</u> — but we may crowd him into a very small space if our hearts are full of other loves:

- love of self
- love of the world and its goodies
- love of human approval
- love of sin
- our own self-righteousness.

His competitors are not only our loves, however, but also

- our worries and fears
- our resentments
- our self-condemnation
- our self-pity
- our superstitions
- our unbelief
- and our distrust of those very teachings which would give a solid foundation to our relationship with Him.

Enabling Him to maximize His presence in our lives involves getting the wrong things out of our hearts — removing hindrances.

And what that has to do with our husbands is the "sometimes we look like a Christian — sometimes we don't" aspect. Our goal is for our husbands to see Christ as often and as clearly as possible when they look at us. He is "the Light" we are to let shine, not by striving to impress our husbands, but by nurturing the presence of Jesus within us.

C. S. Lewis wrote in *Letters to An American Lady* (William B. Eerdmans Publishing Company, Grand Rapids, Michigan, 1967): "How little people know who think that holiness is dull. When one meets the real thing (and perhaps, like you, I have met it only once) it is irresistible. If even 10% of the world's population had it, would not the whole world be converted and happy before a year's end?"

POWER IN PRAYER

The Lord Jesus said in John 15:7, "If ye abide in me and my words abide in you, ye shall ask what ye will, and it shall be done unto you."

There's another precious promise in Psalm 37:3-4: "Trust in the Lord, and do good; so shalt thou dwell in the land, and verily thou shalt be fed. Delight thyself also in the Lord; and he shall give thee the desires of thine heart."

Delighting in the Lord — learning more and more about Him, making Him your best friend and confidant, singing His praises, seeing His loving fingerprints on all your blessings — is our high privilege. The better we get to know Him, the more our desires will coincide with His.

ENJOY YOUR SEPARATION UNTO HIM

Have you ever wished you could trade places with a woman whose husband is a fully-committed Christian, a leader in his home and in the church, a paragon among family men? It's an understandable fantasy for women married to spiritually-dormant men.

Can you believe that there is *anything* enviable in *your* situation?

This is it: our Christian responsibility at this point in our lives is to *build our trust in the Lord and delight ourselves in Him!*

John 15:10-11 says, "If ye keep my commandments, ye shall abide in my love; even as I have kept my Father's commandments, and abide in his love.

"These things I have spoken unto you, that my joy might remain in you, and that your joy might be full."

Look at the differences between us and the mythical woman who might envy us: we are allowed — nay, encouraged — to spend every possible moment in Christ's presence. Our "special scriptures" focus on our character, not our activities: the quiet and gentle spirit, the chaste and respectful way of life, meekness, incorruptibility, lack of fear.

Our counterpart's life necessarily revolves around church events and supporting her husband's Christian service. Leaders and their families are generally present every time the church doors are open, they are expected to volunteer for workdays and visitation programs, to organize, serve and clean up after special meetings, and endless telephone calls interrupt evenings and weekends when there's no church function on the agenda.

That level of busyness can interfere with the pure devotion to Christ that is our recommended portion. We are the "Marys" who are beckoned to sit at Jesus' feet (see Luke 10:39) while we wait for our husbands to join us in our faith. Our character, not our churchwork, is God's chief interest in us.

We have permission to give our devotional life top priority.

So lap up your advantage. Rather than chafing at limited church participation, praise God for this waiting period. Make reading the bible your hobby. Pray without ceasing, even if it has to be done silently. Hunt for opportunities to connect with Him in the odd moments of the day.

Set your own times for worship — which you can do in your pajamas if the opportunity arises during a restless night or while your husband is in the shower.

LIVE A LIFE OF LOVE

When Jesus was asked to name the greatest commandment in the law, He answered: "Thou shalt love the Lord thy God with all thy heart, and with all thy soul, and with all thy mind.

"This is the first and great commandment.

"And the second is like unto it, Thou shalt love thy neighbour as thyself. "On these two commandments hang all the law and the prophets" (see Matthew 22:37-40).

That's the whole program: love God with all you have in you. Then love your neighbor as ardently as you love yourself.

Your husband is surely your closest neighbor.

So in the next chapter, we'll look at that second building project.

LOTTIE'S STORY: COLD COMFORT

Several months after her last visit to church, Lottie came face to face with the pastor in a supermarket aisle.

"Well, Lottie!" he said heartily. "You know, I happened to be driving past your house the other day and I was real tempted to stop in and see you."

Lottie just stared at him.

To give her pastor credit, he probably was "real tempted " to visit Lottie, to inquire why she had stopped coming to church, to encourage her, to pray with her.

But he yielded to a stronger temptation — reluctance to investigate what might prove to be a nasty situation, or even to chance an encounter with The Bogeyman. (If a man will smoke in a church sanctuary, what in the world will he do in his own home?")

EXERCISE 1

ABIDING IN CHRIST: MAKING ROOM FOR THE FULLNESS OF HIS PRESENCE

What unChristlike things occupy space in your heart?
Make a specific list of His competitors. Review and update it regularly.

Sins:

Selfish ambitions — where my will conflicts with God's will:

Affections for things of the world:

Things I need to cast on the Lord, or hide in Him:
worries about:

-
-
-

fears of:

-
-
-

EXERCISE 2

OUR PARTICULAR HINDRANCES TO THE LORD'S ABIDING PRESENCE

Self-condemnation -

- we think maybe the aggravations and limitations of our divided household are punishments from God
- we think we are regarded as second-class citizens in His Kingdom
- we have little sense that we are effectual in prayer
- we have little contentment
- we have little joy

Self-righteousness -

- we feel morally superior to our unbelieving husbands
- we display spiritual pride (the Superstar of sins!)
- we feel resentment against our husbands
- we disrespect him for his lack of belief
- we lose empathy for him
- we resist humbling ourselves under God by submission to him

Self-pity - manifests in

- complaints
- envy of the equally-yoked
- weakening faith
- striving to please people (other than our husbands!)
- lack of fervency in prayer
- lack of endurance

EXERCISE 3

KNOW YOUR ENEMIES!

Self-condemnation -
Comes from looking *back* at our sinful past

Self-righteousness -
Comes from looking *down* at our unbelieving husbands

Self-pity -
Comes from looking *at* others

The remedy:

"Looking unto Jesus, the Author and Finisher of our faith: who for the joy that was set before him endured the cross, despising the shame, and is set down at the right hand of the throne of God. For consider him that endured such contradiction of sinners against himself, lest ye be wearied and faint in your minds "(Hebrews 12:1-2).

His atonement fully satisfied the penalty for our sinful past.

He looks at our husbands with the same love that He has for us.

He is the One to compare ourselves with — and to delight in! He loves us with an everlasting love.

EXERCISE 4

ABIDE — SO YOU MAY BEAR MUCH FRUIT

Eve tempted Adam with forbidden fruit, which led to spiritual death.

Our challenge is to tempt our husbands with the fruit of the Spirit, which leads to eternal life.

Read Galatians 5:22-26. List the fruits of the Spirit

-
-
-
-
-
-
-
-
-

According to verse 24, what have "those who are Christ's" done?

Now read I Peter 3:1-6, and compare the "winning wife's" character traits with the fruits of the Spirit listed above.

Read John 15:1-8.

1. Who is the Husbandman?

2. Who is the True Vine?

3. How important is "fruit" to the Husbandman?

4. According to verse 8, what two things result from our "bearing much fruit"?

CHAPTER 4

Establishing Respect

The Neglected Attitude

LOTTIE'S STORY: 'FOR THE SAKE OF THE CHILDREN'

Lottie was an excellent homemaker and mother. She was also a good wife, if not a very happy one.

It was clear to any onlooker that Bud wore the pants in the family. He "lived large," spending money freely on his wardrobe, a fine car, picking up the tab for friends in the coffeeshop near his agricultural equipment business — and bringing home treats for the family like a whole case of assorted ice cream packed in dry ice, or a sack of melons or nuts he had sweet-talked out of a farmer.

Lottie took care of everything on the home front with a magical touch that stretched the budget to feed and clothe the brood, even when Bud's business began to falter.

Onlookers included her children, who understood the family pecking order. If Lottie said "no," it sometimes meant "maybe," but when Lottie said, "Ask your father," all hope was lost.

They respected him, if their regard was tinged with fear of his impatience. He was The Law.

As for Bud and Lottie, their honeymoon was over. He spent long hours at his shop. Her days were consumed with childcare, laundry and meal preparation.

Lottie occasionally complained about their waning relationship, or about their lack of family life when she couldn't keep her feelings inside any longer.

It always made him defensive — "I'm doing the best I can," he'd snarl. He'd leave the house for hours, and come back enclosed in a bubble of silent anger.

Then Lottie would try not to rock the boat, lest he not come back at all. She could put up with a lot to keep her home intact. Her children were her life.

THE BIGGEST HINDRANCE: LACK OF RESPECT

A household missionary is either the chief architect or an erosive agent in her home.

Proverbs 14:1 says: "Every *wise woman* buildeth her house: but the *foolish* plucketh it down with her hands" (emphasis added).

Since house builders are typically men, this scripture is talking about something beyond the assembly of boards and bricks and plumbing lines and electric wires.

And just as Jesus contrasted the *wise man* who built on rock with the *foolish man* who built on sand, so this scripture contrasts *wisdom* and *foolishness*.

My earthly home
built on the foundation of
UNFALTERING RESPECT FOR MY HUSBAND

For a missionary wife, the integrity of her building project depends on the quality of relationships within the home.

The foundation of a sturdy house is the wife's respect for her husband.

Ephesians 5:33 makes an emphatic directive: "...(let) the wife see that she *reverence* her husband."

DO IT WHETHER HE'S EARNED IT OR NOT

"See that she reverence her husband!"

Isn't reverence an attitude we reserve for God? It seems extreme to expect this of us, particularly the times we experience a husband with still-sleepy crankiness, morning-breath, beard stubble, and pajamas that are overdue for a date with the laundry hamper. Why would God prescribe *reverence* as a way of relating to him?

Surely it is *because* we see him at his least attractive moments. The old adage says, "Familiarity breeds contempt" — and contempt is the antithesis or respect — or reverence.

Lest we suspect that verse was a misprint, Peter chimes in (I Peter 3:5-6): "For after this manner in the old time the holy women also, who trusted in God, adorned themselves, being in subjection unto their own husbands: Even as Sara obeyed Abraham, calling him *lord*..."

So our first directive is to look at our husband with our highest esteem — bestowing on him the highest rank among the mortals in our lives.

The common complaint (yes, I've made it myself many times) is that he doesn't deserve it, that respect is something to be earned and — well, he falls short in lots of ways, particularly in his faith life!

And then to hold up Sarah and Abraham as an example! Abraham was a patriarch, not a pagan! How can I equate my husband with Abraham?

But if we read the account of Abraham's life, we recognize that his behavior wasn't all that shiny.

He asked Sarah to pretend to be his sister, which put her in a compromising position with amorous men. A godly husband would have made her protection his top concern.

And Abraham let Sarah talk him into helping God fulfill His promise to give the aged couple a child. Sarah proposed that Abraham have sex with Hagar, Sarah's maid, and he complied, when a godly husband....

So, if *treating your husband with unfaltering respect as a means to accomplish God's purpose* seems as farfetched as giving birth at age 90 — welcome to the basic faith challenge in winning your husband!

RETURN TO OUR MODEL

If you were a missionary to a foreign population, you wouldn't condemn them for their unChristian ideas and activities. Your wouldn't sneer at their distrust of your beliefs. You would respect them as the people God loved and wanted to include in His family.

You would consider the best ways to influence them to recognize your Savior — and theirs.

RESPECT IS 'GRACE' WE PASS ON

I Peter 4:10 describes Christians who relay what they have received as "good stewards of the manifold grace of God."

Certainly none of us merit the favor God has shown us. We, who deserved death for our sins, have received instead eternal life, adoption into God's own family, and appointment as a joint heir with Jesus Christ: an overwhelming supply of grace. We are clearly "in His good graces" — and our husbands should always be in ours.

Considering what it cost God and His Son to provide such great gifts for us, how can we balk at dispensing the gift of respect to our husbands?

It is a gift that actually costs us nothing, if we suspend our judgments about whether or not he deserves it — and that qualification is something we ought to get rid of, anyway.

AREN'T THERE EXCEPTIONS?

So — are all sorts of "surely not when" examples leaping to mind? (Do I respect him when he's drunk? When he's watching pornography? When he spends his whole paycheck at a gambling hall? When he's taking the Lord's name in vain?)

Of course we don't respect bad *behavior*. But we always respect the bad *behaver.*

We respect his right to make bad choices. God has given him the same free will He gave us.

We allow room for failure. The human nature is weak.

We respect him as a rational being who acts in the particular way he does, for a reason — out of a need for love, for excitement, for recognition, for relief of pain or guilt or stress.

Figuring out what makes him tick is a venture we will undertake as we "look on the field."

We have the advantage of knowing that the Lord Jesus Christ really is the answer to everything we need — but our husbands don't yet believe that.

SO DON'T WE REACT WHEN MEN 'BEHAVE BADLY'?

Of course we do!

It's a good idea, however, to create a policy that we will instantly invoke God into our mouths when we face an unwelcome surprise from our husbands. Then we can (respectfully!) confront him, expressing our disappointment, or dismay, or even anger at his behavior.

We may also have to present an ultimatum to him, if he has done something illegal or dangerous.

Then we shut up, *respecting* his opportunity to say he's sorry — or not to say anything.

Keeping our reaction under the control of the Holy Spirit (another of our big advantages!) will allow that same Holy Spirit to deal with our mate's conscience.

Now, let's look at positive reasons to respect our mates.

HE IS CREATED IN THE IMAGE OF GOD

Your husband is endowed with spiritual possibilities!

He is a product of God's work in Genesis 1:27: "So God created man in his own image, in the image of God created he him; male and female created he them."

Mankind, the crown of God's creation, was invested with a soul, a spirit, a mind, a will, and a conscience.

While Adam's fall into sin put our human race under the curse of death and estrangement from God, God already had a plan in place to rescue His prized creatures. In "the fullness of time," He sent our Savior.

Your husband is eligible for redemption, reconciliation, and restoration. Respect his potential!

GOD VALUES OUR HUSBANDS ENOUGH TO DEDICATE PERSONAL 'MISSIONARIES' TO THEM

Remember how odd it seemed to realize that unbelieving husbands are not generally a prime concern for church outreach?

And the reasons: they rarely wander into a church where they can hear a gospel challenge; they are not a "target group" sought out by go-and-tell teams; and the local church is often ignorant of or not very interested in ways they could partner with a wife in winning her husband.

Then remember those very specialized verses that point to our potential — to be the live-in, living Presence of Christ to him.

RESPECT HIM BECAUSE HE IS GOD'S DEPUTY

Our husbands have God-given roles to perform in our lives.

A husband typically contributes something toward a wife's material needs: food, clothing, shelter, transportation, health care, emergency or retirement funds.

He protects her, not only from a spider in the bathtub or a tricky telemarketer, but he provides a spiritual covering that keeps Satan at bay. He is the *roof* of our spiritual house.

We become targets of spiritual attack when we rebel, or engage in manipulative ploys to circumvent a husband's known wishes — or even when we act presumptiously: following the worldly adage, "It's easier to ask forgiveness than to ask permission."

(Okay, check the copyright date again.)

If you're still with me, consider that your husband is a valuable counselor. He knows you — probably better than you think! — and can sense the rightness or folly of your plans. Pay attention to his reactions: his qualms, questions, or his encouragement.

God will even give your husband spiritual discernment in your behalf.

My friend Jodie came to Christ after she had been married to Darwin for four years. She was totally eager to dive into her new faith.

When a couple of friendly women knocked on her door and offered to help her study the bible with them, it looked like a godsent opportunity to catch up on the years she had missed as a non-churchgoer.

After her first lesson, however, her husband registered several doubts about her new friends and their literature.

Jodie doublechecked Darwin's reservations with a Christian friend, who realized that Jodie was being romanced by a cult. Darwin took the lead to tell the women to suspend their contact with his wife.

Certainly when you face a sorrow or a disappointment, no arms are more comforting than your husband's.

And, obviously, your husband is the only one who can righteously provide you with physical love.

OUR HUSBANDS ARE GOD'S CHIEF AGENTS IN PERFECTING US

God is a master of using a bad situation for good ends.

However you got into a spiritually-divided marriage, God will use your everyday challenges to teach you perseverance and unconditional love — if you allow Him.

According to James 1:5, the *work of patience* while we wait for our husbands to share our belief can make us "perfect and entire, wanting nothing" — if we submit to its process and don't waste the experience.

And what accountability partner could be more effective in holding us to our goals? Who else is going to ask, every time we throw a temper tantrum or badmouth a relative, "Is that how a Christian acts?"

Similar to the way foreign missionaries learn a new language by being totally immersed in the culture, our spiritual formation will take place lickety-split — if we depend on the living Presence of Christ to be our constant companion in our households, and depend on our husbands to keep us on track.

RESPECT IS A BASIC NEED

Sometimes it seems like the scriptures directed to women are degrading — that we are put into a lesser role than our men.

But respect is a basic human need. (Can't you still feel the sting of disrespectful treatment from a store clerk, that persistent telemarketer, a sassy child?)

God insists that we *see to it* that we respect our husbands because our husbands need respect like they need oxygen.

TAKE HIM SERIOUSLY

Once we become Christians, we start to think cosmically — "setting our minds on things above," seeking to live according to God's foreordained purpose for our lives, and looking for God's hand in the affairs of men.

Consequently, we can get a little impatient and dismissive of our husband's earthbound interests and his newscast-formed opinions about the state of the world.

We mustn't.

His career, his hobbies, his friends, and his analyses of how and why things work are important to him, and they must be to us, if we authentically respect him.

REMEMBER THAT HE KNOWS SOME THINGS WE DON'T KNOW

A husband's perception about life is based on his education, relationships, and events he has lived through, which is probably a very different mix than our formative influences.

Respect your husband because he has knowledge, skills and experience you don't have. He's a wonderful resource. Stay on friendly terms with him!

RESPECT HIS GENDER DIFFERENCES

We might as well acknowledge that men and women are wired differently. Some of the complaints we attribute to his unbelieving heart are simply "guy things."

"Guys" do not typically wear their hearts on their sleeves. Even after our husbands receive Christ, they may continue to be emotionally-private — reluctant to talk about feelings and slow to understand how feelings-driven we may be.

They may never become enthusiastic about verbalizing their love for us, just as we may overlook the many ways they try to indicate their love through "works" — killing those spiders, washing our cars, or buying complicated electronic gadgets they think will improve our lives.

They may be slow to risk personal exposure in prayer meetings or small group discussions. It may take a while for them to accept a submissive role in relationship with church leaders.

IS HE RESPECTED EVERYWHERE BUT AT HOME?

The Virtuous Woman of Proverbs 31 is in many ways "the power behind the throne." By keeping her husband's household in good order, she frees his energies for success in his world.

At the other extreme, though, a wife's ingratitude and dissatisfaction, her belittling of him, or undermining his authority, heaps discouragement on her mate. His workplace may then become his place of refuge.

Think about the odd — but not uncommon — situation where a husband is appreciated everywhere but at home. He's ripe pickings for a female associate who would like to take the place of "the wife who doesn't understand him."

RESPECT HIM WITH LITTLE COURTESIES

Say "pardon me" before you interrupt (or better, *don't* interrupt, if you can contain yourself until he's had his say).

Say "please" and "thank you."

Say "I'm sorry" when you've offended him.

Use good table manners.

Neaten the newspaper if he hasn't read it yet. Keep the rooms you share tidy.

Do unto him as you would have him do unto you.

PREFER HIM

We vowed to *forsake all others* when we married.

We are surely scrupulous to avoid romantic entanglements, yet we may spend inordinate time with a female friend, a church clique, or with our parents or siblings.

Certainly it puts too much responsibility on a husband to expect him to meet all your needs for companionship.

But if you have little time left over for him, or are unwilling to rearrange your plans when he suggests a spontaneous getaway, he will feel like he's the one who's been forsaken.

Our husbands belong on the "A list" of the company we keep.

KEEP HIS CONFIDENCES

Duh!

Meeting with a prayer group does not give us a free pass to tattletale, to disparage our husband's dreams, to complain about his habits, or to catalogue his sins.

In fact, the only One who can safely hear what troubles us about any other person is the One who knows all sides of the story, who knows the beginning from the end, and who invites us to unload our cares on Him.

Be very careful what you share about him. Think how powerful words are — people who don't know your husband will form indelible judgments about him from what you tell them. Imagine how negative revelations will affect they way people greet him when you finally get him to go to church with you.

A good rule might be, "Share with others only what you would be willing for him to share about you."

PLEASE LOVE ME — YOU PROMISED YOU WOULD!

You perhaps have heard that, while husbands are commanded to love their wives, scripture nowhere commands women to love their husbands. That's legalistically true. However, older women are told to teach the younger ones to love their husbands and children, so the intent for the husband to be loved by his wife is there.

And, I'll bet you made a vow to love him — before God and witnesses! — during your wedding ceremony.

As an older woman, I see that the bridal love we bring to marriage is actually very conditional.

The world has seen that, too, evidenced by modern vows in which couples promise to stay married "as long as we both shall *love*."

Love that endures is the twin to "respect" — a *chosen attitude* that meets the needs of the beloved over the long haul.

RESPECT IS THE KEY ATTITUDE TO DEVELOP

(Have I mentioned that we need to respect our husbands?)

Sorry to belabor the point, but respect is the KEY to every aspect of marital success. I'm sure you noted that the direction, "let the wife see to it that she respect her husband," is for *all* wives, not just for the unequally-yoked.

So — our spiritual household will have a firm foundation if we build upon unwavering respect for our husbands.

And respect will raise walls of cooperation, confidence, loyalty and trustworthiness — great support for your "spiritual roof."

How else do we build?

Proverbs 24:3-4 tells us, "Through wisdom is an house builded; and by understanding it is established: And by knowledge shall the chambers be filled with all precious and pleasant riches."

Wisdom. Understanding. Knowledge.

Proverbs 4:7 declares: "Wisdom is the principal thing; therefore get wisdom: and with all thy getting get understanding."

The tricky thing is, there's wisdom and there's wisdom: James 3:13-18 describes a *worldly wisdom* generated from envy, strife, sensuality and lies.

Gross examples would be, "Look out for Number One."

"Don't get mad — get even."

"If it feels good, do it."

"Anything goes, as long as it doesn't hurt anybody."

In contrast, "the *wisdom that is from above* is first pure, then peaceable, gentle, and easy to be intreated, full of mercy and good fruits, without partiality, and without hypocrisy. And the fruit of righteousness is sown in peace of them that make peace" (emphasis added).

Do you see the essence of *respect* in "the wisdom from above" — purity, peaceableness, gentleness, easy to approach, full of mercy and good fruits...?

And traits of the wife who may win her husband without a word by her "chaste conversation coupled with fear; " the incorruptible "hidden man of the heart...a meek and quiet spirit."

We live in a miasma of worldly wisdom — among advice columnists, talk-show experts, even movie stars and popular singers who believe that "a smart man is a smart man is a smart man." When someone achieves prominence in a performing art, we suddenly provide them audience to speak on any subject at all, and consider their opinions authoritative.

So how do we get the real thing?

Obviously, we start in God's word, where we get a crystal-clear definition: "The fear of the Lord is the beginning of wisdom, and the knowledge of the holy is understanding" (Proverbs 9:10).

That devotional life again — sitting at Jesus' feet every chance we get, practicing His presence in every situation, attending with utmost seriousness to His teachings. Developing a quiet spirit and beautifying the "hidden man of the heart."

⁂

LOTTIE'S STORY: LIVING HER MARITAL VOW

When Bud's business venture didn't succeed as well as he had hoped, he went to work as a travelling salesman, and selling turned out to be his forte. He liked dressing to impress, and he liked driving the long distances across the southwest with no company but the radio.

Five days a week on the road took its toll, however. When Bud came home, he was exhausted and in no mood for the noise generated by active children.

Under Lottie's coaching, a rule of silence prevailed when Bud pulled into the driveway on Friday night, and lifted when he took off to hunt or fish with friends, or to hang out at the airport, where he was taking flying lessons — or until he drove off again on Monday morning.

Life was no longer fun for Lottie.

When Bud was off on his trips and loneliness overwhelmed her, she would put the younger kids to bed and sit on Harriet's bedside. Instead of bedtime bible stories, the mother and daughter talked about Lottie's disappointments and discouragement in her marriage.

"Why don't we divorce him?" Harriet suggested.

Lottie stiffened, and her hazel eyes flashed. "He once asked me if I wanted a divorce. I told him, no, that marriage means something to *me*."

Harriet thought about that. Life was not much fun for her and her siblings when Bud was at home, either. She longed to have a dad like her friends', who still pulled their "little girls" onto their laps or held their hands when they went for a walk, or noticed when they had a new hairstyle. A dad to be close to.

She was glad she had a mother who was twice as good as anyone else's.

EXERCISE 1

GETTING DOWN TO BUSINESS:
MAKING MY HOME A PLACE OF MINISTRY

A. What are the functions of a house?

- physical shelter
- place to be nourished
- place to rest
- place to practice hospitality

(what else?):

-
-
-
-

B. Review Proverbs 14:1. What kind of wife builds her house? With whom is she contrasted?

C. Read Psalm 127:1. Who must be her co-builder?

D. Review Proverbs 24:3-4. What building materials does the house-builder use?

- With what does she furnish her home?

E. Think of some "precious and pleasant riches" with which you can furnish your home:

- trust
- open communication
- order
- peace
-
-
-
-

Happy decorating!

EXERCISE 2

HOW WELL DOES MY HOME REPRESENT THE KINGDOM OF GOD?

In peace:

- material sources of conflict (TV, shared bathrooms, computer use, etc.)
- attitudes: rebellion, argumentativeness, aggression, selfishness
-
-

In love:

- emotional tone
- level of courtesy
- demonstrations of affection
- willingness to serve one another
-
-

In joy:

- planned (or neglected) family activities
- sharing of each other's successes and comforting one another's sorrows
- shared laughter
-
-

In order:

- are possessions well maintained and kept in assigned places?
- is cooperation a paramount attitude among family members?
- are life-skills — responsibility, time and resource management, etc. — being taught and practiced by your children?
-
-

In hospitality: how welcome are friends

- to telephone
- to visit

- to share a meal or stay overnight
- to borrow your things?

What improvements would you like to make?

How will you accomplish them?

EXERCISE 3
PREPARING THE WAY OF THE LORD: REMOVING HINDRANCES BETWEEN OURSELVES AND OUR HUSBANDS

What does "respect" include?

How do you demonstrate respect?

How do you demonstrate lack of respect?

What part does your self-respect play in interactions with your husband?

When do I have problems showing respect?
- when I judge him
- when I visit my arsenal of grudges
- when he disrespects me
- other:

What might these problems point to in my life?
- pride
- unforgiveness
- bitterness
-

What can I do to change things for the better?

EXERCISE 4

BIDING TIME: WHAT IS GOD TEACHING ME THROUGH THE DISCIPLINE OF GIVING RESPECT?

- humility
- how to "deny myself," or "lay down my life"
- gratitude
- recognition of His sovereignty
- the essence of unconditional love: meeting needs regardless of the needy one's merits
-
-
-

Make it your daily prayer and your daily practice to seek God's help in building respect in your home.
When you experience an "aha!" moment, record it in your journal.

EXERCISE 5

LET PATIENCE HAVE HER PERFECT WORK

Read James 1:2-4.

- How are we supposed to greet our trials ("diverse temptations" in KJV)?

- Why?

- What will the process of patience-development do for us?

Read Galatians 5:22-23.

- what does this scripture say about patience ("longsuffering" in KJV)?

Read I Peter 1:6-7.

- What else will be produced by trials?

Read I Peter 4:12-16.

- What else will happen when we are tried?

Read 2 Peter 3:8-9.

- What is God's attitude toward an unbeliever?

Can you also be patient with your unbeliever? Turn joyfully to God when your days of waiting seem like a thousand years!

CHAPTER 5

Clarifying Priorities

What *Should* You Neglect?

THE FRUIT OF BITTERNESS

Lottie's withdrawal affected her whole family's attitude toward church and, to some extent, toward God. As Hebrews 12:15 describes, a "root of bitterness" sprang up.

Lottie longed for the same warmth she had enjoyed in the church she grew up in, where her parents and siblings were all churchgoers.

But when marriage and her new social life took priority, her long-standing discipline of church attendance dissolved.

She valiantly tried to rebuild the habit, but the added burden of children to dress, transport, and then distribute to the nursery and their various Sunday school classes before she arrived — usually late — to her own class, then collecting everybody afterwards, prevented her from lingering to chat with other people, who didn't seem overly interested in her, anyway. They had their own favorite friends to catch up with before church service started.

The kids were willing to go to Sunday school as long as Lottie was willing to take them, but none except 11-year-old Harriet wanted to stay for church. The pastor's daughter was Harriet's current best friend, and they had been allowed to become junior members of the choir. Lottie did her best to avoid complaining about having to make a second trip to pick up her firstborn after worship service.

Bud, of course, cynically claimed to have known all along that church people were a bunch of hypocrites, and Lottie's experience confirmed it. If the kids still wanted to go to Sunday school, that was all right with him. It gave him a little bit of peace and quiet on Sunday mornings.

Lottie loved her children passionately. They were her world, now. And her marriage was at least fruitful. After a break of several years, she and Bud had two more daughters.

Lottie didn't baptize them.

HARRIET'S STORY: AN ENTHUSIASTIC 'CHURCHIAN'

Harriet, Lottie and Bud's firstborn, loved Sunday school. It was her first social experience outside the family. She enjoyed the pictures to color, the simple craft projects, the flannel-board stories.

She and Lottie sang "Jesus Loves Me" together at bedtime every night. Harriet took turns relating Sunday school stories with the ones Lottie read to her from her children's books.

Before she could name all the days of the week, she knew that Sunday was her favorite.

She was very much at home in church.

So much so that it didn't disturb her when her mother quietly withdrew from church attendance. Lottie still took Harriet and her siblings to Sunday school, and she allowed Harriet, then eleven years old, to stay for church.

In eighth-grade, however, Harriet changed schools and found a new best friend, who attended another church — the same denomination Bud had attended as a child.

She decided to visit there, since her friend's parents were willing to pick her up Sunday mornings, and it became her new church home. Her siblings slowly abandoned their Sunday school.

Harriet's tranfer to his denomination made no difference to Bud. Nor did Lottie have any interest in seeing how another congregation might have treated her.

Harriet was an enthusiastic "churchian" as a teenager, joining the youth group and the junior women's circle. A great place to find nice friends.

After high school, she went to work at a distant university affiliated with her chosen denomination, and eventually enrolled for classes as well — although she didn't go to church at all anymore. She had plenty of friends in college.

Her new friendships revolved around weekend parties rather than church activities — exciting, "forbidden territory" compared to the life she led in her hometown. A little disturbing to her conscience, but she was old enough to make her own decisions.

Ironically, campus was where Harriet made her first spiritual decision. It happened in a sociology class, when a classmate gave the rationale for his atheism.

Harriet had been shocked at first, but as she thought over the young man's argument, she tried it on for size. She found a huge burden lift from her heart. The inconsistencies of the two different lives she had lived no longer troubled her if there was No One to hold her to account.

She eventually returned to her hometown to attend the local state college.

And met her future husband.

His childhood church had built strong habits (although no real belief) into him.

He had been on his own for several years, working to save money to go to college fulltime. He had long ago left his religious heritage behind him.

When they decided to marry, Harriet suggested they hold the wedding at the church she had attended years before.

The pastor graciously overlooked Harriet's long defection from church, but required that she and her fiance meet with him for premarital counseling.

They complied, more or less tongue-in-cheek. The only memorable part of their three sessions was the pastor's concern about the difference in their church backgrounds. Although Harriet's fiance declared his church involvement was "history," the pastor insisted that those early influences could surface in the future.

He offered Harriet a booklet to acquaint her with the beliefs of her fiance's family. She skimmed it, and laughed it off. While her fiance only claimed to be an agnostic rather than an atheist, they agreed that faith would not be one of their problems.

Fast forward eight years. Harriet lived in California, still married, but not happily — nothing about her life was happy.

She faced a writing deadline which had kept her up until early morning, and she struggled out of bed a few hours later to finish the last pages. It was Saturday, and she needed to catch the mail carrier before noon.

With the final page in hand, she froze. Her back refused to do her bidding, and she had to have her husband's help to get up from her chair.

Late on a Saturday morning, there was no chance of being "worked in" at her doctor's office. Even if she could see him, his remedy would be muscle relaxants, which would take several days to provide relief.

She had never felt so immobilized. Every movement sent shock waves of pain through her back.

Harriet asked her husband to check the telephone book for a chiropractor. The compassionate receptionist who answered his phone call said, "Come in and wait."

Her husband helped Harriet into the reception room, where they were greeted by a life-size portrait of Jesus Christ. The tables were stacked with Christian magazines and evangelical tracts. Harriet rolled her eyes at her husband. But they waited.

A long wait, until the chiropractor had treated all the people who had appointments. Following a short examination, he adjusted her spine, which gave Harriet instant relief.

"I'm glad that helped," the chiropractor said, "but I recommend that we keep on treating you for a few weeks to protect against a recurrence."

The very next treatment, the chiropractor inquired about Harriet's faith. In view of his obvious dedication to Christ, Harriet gave an evasive answer. He told her what he had read in his morning devotions and how it made him so grateful for Christ's work in his life.

So it went, treatment after treatment, the chiropractor talking about Christ and Harriet offering no disagreement. She even made a few tepid comments she remembered from her teenage churchgoing days.

And she began to evaluate her "commitment" to atheism. She realized that in her early church years, she had not understood who Christ was, or what His death meant.

She had never read the bible, beyond the short passages presented in a Sunday school lesson or youth devotional.

Her prayers were rote formulas she had learned as a young child, with a few "help me!"s thrown in.

During her next back treatment, she confessed she really didn't know much about the bible. The chiropractor suggested that she read the Gospel of John, then his three epistles: I John, II John and III John.

As soon as she got home, she made an all-out search for the small bible she had received as a Sunday school attendance award years before. She sat at her dining room table and began to read.

John's gospel was difficult, but she plowed through, a few chapters a day, until she finished the gospel and started the first epistle.

When she reached I John 4:8, she nearly gave it up. "He that loveth not knoweth not God, for God is love."

How could she have turned away from Him? No wonder her life had taken such a downturn. She didn't know love. She didn't know Love.

But she read on. Verse 9 was almost a paraphrase of John 3:16: "In this was manifested the love of God toward us, because that God sent his only begotten Son into the world, that we might live through him."

She had actually memorized John 3:16 as a child. Why hadn't she realized what it meant? And WHY DIDN'T SHE LOVE GOD?

I John 4:10 changed her life. "Herein is love, *not that we loved God*, but that *he loved us*, and sent his Son to be the propitiation for our sins" (emphasis added).

She sank to the floor on her knees and cried like she had never cried before: tears of repentance, tears of commitment, tears of relief, tears of joy — tears of love.

She could hardly wait to get back to church!

"I just became a Christian," she told her husband when he came home from work.

He stared at her. "How do you know?" he asked.

"I asked Jesus to forgive my sins, and I know He did because of what the bible says."

Her husband continued to stare at her. "What's for supper?" he asked.

She drove to her chiropractor's church the next Sunday — and suddenly felt totally intimidated by the huge building. She didn't know anyone there but the chiropractor. And he wasn't expecting her.

She sat in her car, staring at the front door. She had just put her key back in the ignition, planning to go home, when a pretty woman knocked on her passenger window.

"Hi! Are you a newcomer? Come in and sit with us."

Harriet got out of her car and introduced herself to Myra and her husband, Dean. Harriet discovered they lived a few blocks from her home.

After service, the couple walked Harriet to her car. "Why don't you come with me to a child evangelism class that's starting next Sunday?" Myra suggested. "We'll pick you up."

The class provided training for "Backyard Clubs," a form of vacation bible school held in neighborhoods.

Myra proposed that she and Harriet volunteer to host a club — and when they got back home, Myra assessed that Harriet's backyard was more suitable than hers.

So, by Harriet's second visit to a church, she was involved in churchwork.

A few weeks later, Harriet's home became a mission site for neighborhood children.

Elated from the successful summer project, Harriet filled her schedule with church activities: Sunday school, morning and evening service on Sundays and bible study Wednesday nights.

Her husband, too stunned at first to raise an objection, began to complain. "We can never do anything on weekends anymore, since you're always in church," he said.

Harriet was astounded. Her husband routinely spent most of his weekends at an airport, flying or working on his small plane. Why was their lack of togetherness suddenly her fault?

A godly friend advised her to back off from church for a while. After much deliberation, Harriet decided to take a one-year sabbatical.

There followed an initial flurry of weekend activities, then her husband resumed his own hobbies, leaving Harriet to sit at home, watching religious television programs with pursed lips and a resentful heart.

At the end of her self-imposed exile, Harriet reasserted her desire to go to church again. She told her husband she would also like to enroll in a newly-offered bible study program offered at the church two evenings a week.

Her husband suggested she consider a bible college in a neighboring town instead, where she could attend classes in daytime. The college was 40 miles from home, and affiliated with a denomination she knew nothing about. Going there turned out to be one of the greatest blessings of Harriet's life — attending morning chapel, then serious study of scripture with earnest young Christians. But before she had completed her second week of classes, the student employment office called her in.

"We notice you commute to school," the advisor began. "One of our churches about halfway between the college and your home needs a secretary. Would you be interested in interviewing?"

The pastor hired Harriet on the spot, agreeing to grant her time to attend chapel and her bible college class until the end of the semester. Harriet felt she had gone from glory to glory.

What more could she want, than to be a helper to a holy man of God?

Over the years, Harriet was ever the moth, churchwork ever the flame. Her husband spent more and more time at the airport. Aviation was his religion.

For a time he went to church with her for special musical presentations and to Sunday school social events, but he suddenly refused an invitation with the statement: "I am never, under any circumstances, going to set foot in a church again."

Harriet was crushed. She had thought he was slowly warming to the exciting life she led.

Well — God certainly had plenty of work for her to do while she waited for Him to do something about her husband's salvation.

CHURCH IS IMPORTANT TO US FOR MANY RIGHT REASONS

We need a church connection.

A church is a place to pool resources. When we add our monetary gifts to a larger fund, the organization can accomplish greater works in the world beyond our homes than we can do as individuals.

We need a place to receive discipleship — systematic bible teaching from the pulpit or in a Sunday school class.

Hearing the prayers of a pastor, teacher or other laymen helps our prayer lives grow. Worshipping with other believers is an enriching experience that we ought to share as frequently as practical.

A local church is a place to give and receive encouragement, even if it's only friendly chitchat before and after service. Interacting with other believers strengthens our sense of identity with Christ's Body.

A local church is the right venue for three important steps of obedience:

1. It is the ideal place to make a public declaration of faith, or of recommitment to the Lord (see Romans 10:9-10).

2. If you have never been baptized, a church service is a good place to follow our Lord in this meaningful sacrament (see Mark 1:4-11).

3. Another important sacrament is the Lord's Supper. Denominational

churches vary in the frequency with which they offer communion. If you have to ration your church visits, try to schedule them when you can partake of this symbolic meal.

Receiving the "Lord's Supper" is a valuable time for personal reflection, to remember the price that was paid for your salvation and for your admission into the fellowship of believers. It is also a time to reaffirm your mystical connection to those with whom you share the bread and the cup.

How much more meaningful would it have been for Lottie, had her children been baptized among a community of friends, by a pastor who had prayed for her during her pregnancies? How might she have been treated with more concern and helpfulness by churchgoers, had she made a recommitment of faith among them? How might the root of bitterness have withered, had she determined to feed at the Lord's Table occasionally?

THE CHURCH IS BOTH A RESOURCE AND A REFINING TOOL

Other situations may arise where a pastoral connection is desirable: funeral services, grave illness, for spiritual counsel, or when we become one of "the needy" the church is designed to help.

Assembling with other believers enables us to keep our problems in perspective — other Christians face situations, many much more devastating than ours, with grace and courage.

We also exult in the gifts our brothers and sisters demonstrate — their wisdom, their devotion, their power in prayer. We get to bask in, as well as generate, the example of Christian light.

And when we engage in small group activities or work days, we experience a different kind of "love laboratory" than the one at home: the more deeply connected we are with other believers, the more we will hone each other through conflicts — which may lead to the disciplinary procedures prescribed when church people tangle with each other.

WHEN CHURCH IS IMPORTANT FOR WRONG REASONS

Sometimes devotion to church activities is an easier path than staying home and doing the difficult work of building a winning relationship with a mate. Church relationships are much more antiseptic — you can back away from them when they become unpleasant.

Church is also an easier place to "let your light shine" than at home. We can become quite addicted to the approval of brethren who admire *our* gifts, *our* patience, *our* power in prayer.

We can even develop a love for their pity over our divided marriage, the sweetheart banquets we have to decline, their suspicions that our bright smiles hide broken hearts.

As in Harriet's story, churchwork can seduce us away from our mission fields. The modern emphasis on discovering spiritual gifts and living a purposeful life makes sitting at home with an unbeliever seem like wasted time.

Some of us would much rather be, like Jesus, "in the temple, sitting in the midst of the doctors, both hearing them, and asking them questions" (Luke 4:46).

Surely, we reason, if we stay close to the center of holy activity, we'll have greater influence with God. Surely if we fold church bulletins, answer the church phones, straighten out the pastor's filing cabinet, wash the nursery linens, decorate tables for the youth banquet, God will take notice.

And if gifts of money to the church cause dissension with our husbands, we may feel obliged to bless the congregation with our time and energy instead.

(Please refer again to the subhead of this section.)

CHURCH CAN BE THE CHIEF HINDRANCE FOR YOUR MATE

If your husband dissuades you from giving funds to a church, don't commit to spending time instead of money. If that substitution was a good idea, God would have mentioned it as an option in His word.

Recognize that following your husband's preference is one way to respect him. God may change his heart in good time, and then you can both give *cheerfully* — which God loves, according to II Corinthians 9:7. (Do you think He loves gifts which are made deceptively, or in opposition to the one you are trying to win?)

Overspending time and energy at church hinders the development of a "winning relationship" at home. It fosters resentment in our husbands.

We need to choose all our expenditures — time, energy, emotion, and money — carefully, when we divert resources that our husbands feel belong to them.

WHY YOUR HUSBAND SHOULD BE INVOLVED IN YOUR CHOICE OF A CHURCH

Membership in a local church is a source of contention for many people, not just unequally-yoked wives. Many people feel you shouldn't have to join (or even attend!) a local church to worship God.

Church leaders desire to add numbers to their rolls, and formal membership gives them a number they can count on. The "people-pleasing" nature — in women, particularly — yearns to take that step.

But it involves commitment. Membership is usually formalized by an exchange of vows between the member and the church body: the member promises to support the church with time, treasure and loyalty. The church promises nurture and inclusion. Voting rights and eligibility for holding leadership positions are bestowed.

So what's the problem?

If you expect your husband to join you in the church you have chosen, you add another uphill stretch to your struggle. You have usurped his leadership by committing to a body of people, a style of worship, a pastoral personality which may not suit him at all.

Another serious consideration he will have is: what negative things do they know about him? He has undoubtedly been an object of prayer and possibly of counsel — how would you feel about going someplace where "your reputation had preceded you"?

The Old Testament actually addresses the making of vows by a wife apart from her husband's authority, in Numbers 30:6-8: "And if she had at all an husband, when she vowed, or uttered ought out of her lips, wherewith she bound her soul;

"and her husband heard it, and held his peace at her in the day that he heard it, then her vows shall stand, and her bonds wherewith she bound her soul shall stand.

"But if her husband disallowed her on the day that he heard it; then he shall make her vow which she vowed, and that which she uttered with her lips, wherewith she bound her soul, of none effect: and the Lord shall forgive her."

If you haven't already formalized membership with a church, defer. If you feel pressured to join, explain that you are waiting for your husband's participation before you make a commitment you may have to break.

This may seem like a moot point. Why should your husband care whether or not you join the church — he's mad simply because you attend!

But think about how the poor pastor, and the members of his congregation will feel if you have to back out. Their emotions are a small-scale analogy to that of someone being served divorce papers. You will also suffer — breaking a vow is a whopping failure.

Consider calling yourself an "adherent," which is an informal attachment to a particular church body. Let the pastor know that you will attend as faithfully as possible, but that your ongoing association is dependent on your husband's pleasure.

Please wait for your husband — your spiritual head — before you make a "soul-binding agreement" to a local church.

The absence of voting rights and ineligibility to hold church office may also help you restrain the amount of time you spend away from your true site of ministry.

DISTINGUISH BETWEEN 'CHRIST'S CHURCH' AND 'MY CHURCH'

As you know, we become eternal members of Christ's church — the supernatural organism of all believers across time and space — when we commit our lives to Him. I Peter 2:5-6 describes us as "living stones," being built up into a spiritual house whose Cornerstone is the Lord Jesus Himself.

The church we *attend* is a small representation of that universal church. In the first century, Paul addressed the people he wrote to as "the church at Ephesus," for example — the believers in a geographical locale.

A local church today, however, may be only one of a huge number of gathering places. My sister lives in a town with a population of 300 — and four churches. My mid-sized town lists more than 100 churches in the Yellow Pages.

So, even if your *local church* involvement is slim to none, you are a fully-qualified member of Christ's eternal Church.

If your attendance at weekend services aggravates your husband, investigate whether a local church offers take-home tapes or CDs of their services, or if they transmit on radio, television, or on a website. Perhaps you or a friend could record broadcast services for playback at your convenience.

PARACHURCH MINISTRIES: YES OR NO?

Parachurch ministries offer "church-like" options: several interdenominational bible study groups offer weekday or evening classes in metropolitan areas. Some which have stood the test of time are Bible Study Fellowship, Precept Ministries, and the Bethel Bible Series. Be aware, however, that they require commitment — not "drop in when you have a chance." (That's a good policy, by the way — a methodical teaching series needs to be received in an orderly manner.)

Radio and television ministries can also provide systematic teaching or preaching, and often will include special music as well to add a worship experience. Again, you can record the programs and play them at the best time for you.

If you are a new Christian, check with a pastor or a mature friend in the faith to assure that the television personality you have in mind is a respected teacher with a balanced ministry.

CHOOSE YOUR 'HEROES' CAREFULLY

Radio and television outreach, like an institutional church, requires funds to operate. Be aware that if you send offerings to a broadcast minister, or purchase his products, you will receive mailings that may create friction at home — the "they are after your money" claim.

One day my postal carrier had tried to deliver a piece of certified mail — which required a signature — while my husband and I were both at work. The notice gave us the option of picking it up at the post office during business hours.

Curiosity burned. I worked a long distance from our local post office. My sweet husband's office was closer, so he offered to pick up the mail during his lunch hour the next day.

He stood in line quite a while to retrieve the letter. He was as curious as I to see what important information he had brought home.

I opened the envelope and found an "emergency appeal" from a televangelist I had sent offerings to in the past, asking for a special, sacrificial gift to keep him on the air in our area.

He had sent out the expensive mailing to make sure he got his addressees' attention.

He got my husband's attention, all right.

Other drawbacks to considering a broadcast personality as a substitute pastor are: he knows nothing about you, your needs, your home situation. He will not be available to perform your baptism or a family funeral.

But the airwaves can provide good teaching and preaching if you conduct a patient search. I once worked where I had a 45-minute commute, and two radio teachers made my long drives the favorite times of my day.

'SPIRITUAL MARY' AND 'PRACTICAL MARTHA'

Church attendance versus spending time with a husband is just one of our priority problems.

For household missionaries, our "abundant life" comprises a double existence: a Christ-centered life, with its call to abide in Him, and a husband-centered home and social life, with its call to serve his needs.

Among Jesus' close friends was a family He stayed with when He visited their village. Martha (a historical "Martha Stewart" prototype) majored in hospitality. Luke 10:38-42 records:

"...Martha received him into her house. And she had a sister called Mary, which also sat at Jesus' feet, and heard his word.

"But Martha was cumbered about much serving, and came to him, and said, Lord, dost thou not care that my sister hath left me to serve alone? bid her therefore that she help me.

"And Jesus answered and said unto her, 'Martha, Martha, thou are careful and troubled about many things;

"'But one thing is needful: and Mary hath chosen that good part, which shall not be taken away from her.'"

These sisters highlight the two-fold challenge of a household missionary: our Lord indicates that sitting at His feet, hearing His word, is "that good part."

Our husbands, however, are interested in our "troubling about many things," like caring for our homes, getting our cars serviced on schedule, stocking the cupboards, preparing meals....They have legitimate grievances when our spiritual life (and particularly our church life) inconveniences them.

It's a tough balancing act, (one which all Christian wives face, by the way). But we can remove some of our husbands' opposition if we give essential priority to our household service — and we can assure ourselves of time for our devotional practices if we define which things are worth troubling about and which are not.

THE PRIMACY OF SPIRITUAL DISCIPLINES

I once worked for a busy executive with whom I exchanged reminders in passing as we went about our separate tasks. It was a difficult challenge to squeeze in time for a formal exchange of information.

But when we did, I gained new insights into my boss's aims and business philosophy. He transferred new responsibilities to me when he had focussed time to explain what he wanted me to do.

Our mission model presents a similar situation: if we were on a foreign field, frequent communication with headquarters would be key to our success. Headquarters would be the source of our material supply, encouragement, direction. Our urgent e-mails would surely get quick attention — but a well-run mission outpost would also put thoughtful time into "looking on the field," reviewing objectives, celebrating victories, specifying needs.

The Lord God is our Headquarters. We need to schedule a time of interchange with Him daily — to review our objectives: His Kingdom and His righteousness; to discern how we can fulfill His will in our little patch of the earth; to cast on Him the cares and puzzles that weigh us down; to state our needs, interceding for our families and asking His wisdom in how to draw them closer to Him.

If you have to neglect something, don't let it be prayer.

Equally important is our need for systematic teaching. We will never learn to "rightly divide the word of truth" as II Timothy 2:15 recommends if our bible study is hit or miss, if we church-hop, if we feel duty bound to read every book a friend offers to lend us, or if we limit our bible reading time to familiar and favorite passages.

The bible is our best textbook. Give priority to reading it, if you have to choose between reading God's word and reading a book *about* the bible.

Many bibles include a reading program to take you through the whole text in a year. It's certainly worthwhile to do that at least once in your life.

I have found it exciting to read the bible cover to cover every year. It is such a big book that I never tire of it, and after more than 30 readings, it still holds fresh discoveries.

Mere reading is not *study*, however. A pastor or Sunday school leader who teaches verse-by-verse, or a multi-week series on a particular book of the bible can supply a deeper grasp of scripture.

A published workbook on biblical prayers, the parables or miracles of Jesus, or — well, spiritual disciplines — can also provide the equipping we need for our lonely ministry.

SAY 'NO' TO THE 'YES SYNDROME'

Church work isn't the only competitor for the time we need for personal devotions and our marital responsibilities. Our "people-pleasing" natures make us appealing targets for other organizations, family members, and friends to ask for our time and work.

I'll admit, I hate to disappoint people, to refuse to meet an expressed need.

But I often say "yes" without determining whether the new opportunity is a work God has appointed for me, or a distraction from the *one thing* He wants to receive my focus.

Knowing what God wants from me is a solid foundation for decision-making, for keeping my best self available and fresh for His priorities.

Instead of automatically saying "yes," ask for a delay to give your answer, then pray for direction (and for resolve, if God's answer is to decline).

One last culprit can seduce you away from your priorities: yourself. Regularly inventory how much time you give every week to television, reading novels, idle chatter on the telephone or e-mail, sitting and staring, or whatever practices eat away at your calendar.

DAILY I WILL PAY MY VOWS

God is pretty fussy about vows, even the casual commitments we make to all those people who want a piece of our time and energy. When we say we'll do something, integrity demands that we follow through.

So before you make a new promise, take care of the two important ones already in place: your commitment to follow Christ, and your marital commitment.

Joni Eareckson Tada reported in *Discipleship Journal* (January/February 2007) that she preaches the gospel to herself every morning. She continued: "I also ask God, 'What is my mission today? What fresh things about Yourself will You show me?' It's really the only way to wake up."

That seems to me like a good way to set the day's agenda in the context of what we're all about: redeemed sinners responding to what Christ has done for us by doing the good works God has ordained for us.

After turning your eyes upon Jesus, spare a glance for the fellow beside you whom you have vowed to love and honor. What tasks will that involve today?

HIS FRIENDS, MY FRIENDS, OUR FRIENDS

Has your commitment to Christ caused a social division in your marriage? Another source of resentment over a wife's faith is that a husband's unbelieving friends lose status — and possibly a sense of welcome — in his home.

Consider whether you have downgraded your interest in your husband's friends, who used to think of you as "one of their own" before your preferences turned toward Christian friends.

Now consider those Christian friends, whom your husband may treat disrespectfully, or whose claims on your time are a source of resentment for him. Your excitement over "the right kind of friends" may be a hindrance you'll have to deal with in preparing the way of the Lord to your husband's heart.

Return to our model. If you were a foreign missionary, ministering to a likely convert, how would you treat the people he cared about? And would you prefer to spend your time with other missionaries, rather than with him?

~

LOTTIE AND BUD: FLASHBACK — CHANGES

Lottie counted on Harriet for help with childcare from the time her second child was born. Harriet loved being a "little mother."

As a "girlfriend," Harriet had little wisdom to offer when Lottie would unload on her — but she was a good listener, and that was what Lottie needed.

She also unfailingly took Lottie's side in every issue.

As for Bud, he had never been an affectionate parent to his kids when they were small — but as the boys grew old enough to fish, hunt, and hike, he included them in his weekend adventures. He even quit smoking when he had trouble matching their stamina.

Then he found a marvelous vehicle: a huge, burly power wagon with four-wheel drive and three rows of seats. He loaded it with a tent, a camp-stove, kerosene lanterns, cots and sleeping bags — and his family. Off they went, almost every weekend from late spring through early autumn. Together at last.

Lottie actually enjoyed the camping trips, exploring the forests and water courses, the Indian ruins and ghost towns of their state. Their adventures gave her greater access to her beloved sons, and Bud was fun to be with again.

EXERCISE 1
A PRACTICAL EXERCISE IN SETTING PRIORITIES

Living an "abundant life" means we have many activities to juggle. Re-read the story of Martha and Mary in Luke 10:38-42, then consider how our dual roles of disciple and missionary wife compare with those of the sisters.

List the disciplines and tasks you currently perform, or would like to accomplish, in your two roles.

Then prayerfully evaluate: which are the important, or "necessary" activities we need to perform in each role?

What are you neglecting? What are you overdoing? Which tasks are most important to the Lord? To your husband? Only to you?

The disciplines of spiritual Mary

-
-
-
-
-
-

The tasks of practical Martha

-
-
-
-
-
-

How can you streamline your lists — and your schedule?

EXERCISE 2
CHRIST'S CHURCH, MY CHURCH

Christ's church is His "new creation," and includes all people across time and space who have placed their faith in His atoning sacrifice for their sin.

Obviously, the church you attend is a "church within the Church." How do the two differ?

Christ's Church	My local church
• an organism (His Body)	• an organization
• all believers historically and globally	• live people who meet at a local address
• led by Christ	• led by pastor & deacons under Christ's authority
• grows through dispersion	• grows through gathering
• transcends culture	• impacts (or may conform to!) culture
•	•
•	•
•	•
•	•
•	
•	

EXERCISE 3
SELF-DISCOVERY AND PRAYER PROJECT: CHRIST'S CHURCH, LOCAL CHURCH - PART 2

1. How am I securely a part of "Christ's church" regardless of my participation in a local church?

2. What are my advantages as a participant in a local church?

3. What are my responsibilities, under Christ, to a local church?

4. Does "my church" compete in any way with my husband's need for my time, affection, attention?

5. Am I looking to "my church" for emotional and ego satisfaction I should find from my family or directly from my Lord?

6. Do I have any confusion about these two concepts? Any hindering dependence on "my church" as opposed to the church my husband might prefer?

7. Have I inadvertently been trying to convert my husband to 'my church' rather than to the Lord Jesus Christ?

Pray about your answers.

EXERCISE 4
MAXIMIZE YOUR ASSETS:
HIS FRIENDS, MY FRIENDS, OUR FRIENDS

Develop a prayer list of your husband's friends, and begin to consider them an auxiliary mission field: people you will respect, serve, and welcome into your home.

Prepare an "arsenal of blessings" for them. When one of "his friends" drops by, make a pot of coffee or a bowl of microwave popcorn. Ask a question or two about his family, his job or his hobby. (Then leave the men to their own conversation while you take advantage of the time for personal devotions!)

Pray for wisdom as to how you can unobjectionably maintain — or if necessary, limit — your separate social circle of Christian friends.

How could you blend his friends and your friends into joint social activities?

- Try out a new restaurant together?
- Host a holiday cookout at your home?
-
-

Jot down ideas where there is a common thread of interest between your husband and your favorite friends.

-
-
-

EXERCISE 5
LOVE YOUR LIMITS!

We have looked at a small number of scriptures that are addressed to women in previous exercises. As you read through the bible, be alert for other scriptures addressed to or describing women and for other distinctions that currently apply to you:

Family:
- parent
- child
- wife
- sibling
-

Master/slave! (workplace, household services)
- employer
- employee

Ministry gifts:
- helper
- gift of serving
- leadership
- teaching
- giving
-

- What kind of church would Christ have if everybody dabbled with every task?
- What is enhanced when specific duties are delegated to designated groups?
- Think of the modern synonym for limits: boundaries. What are the virtues of "knowing the boundaries"?
- Now think of *focus* as a synonym for limits. What would that imply for success in any endeavor?

CHAPTER 6

The Dreaded 'S' Words: Submission, Sacrifice, Suffering

The Neglected Dynamics

HARRIET'S STORY: FLASHBACK

Harriet was the one to move out from the family circle, and church was the divider. She was old enough to drive, and she much preferred going to youth group events and Sunday church services over roughing it at a campsite with her family.

There was one "roughing" experience she liked, however — the annual sleepover with her junior women's circle in Mrs. See's lovely backyard.

Mrs. See, the sponsor of her circle, was the widow of a preacher who had died en route to his assignment in New Mexico.

With two young daughters in tow, Mrs. See decided to complete the trip and make their home in the appointed destination.

She took a job teaching mathematics in the local high school, reared her girls, and when they were launched on their own, she fulfilled her lifelong dream of learning to fly.

And fly she did. All the way to Alaska and back, solo. All over the country to paint runway numbers at small airports with a women pilots' organization — and to race in the women's Powder Puff Derby. A fabulous woman, someone Harriet loved and admired.

But Harriet's senior year in high school was also graduation year from junior women's circle. During their last sleepover, the seniors chomped Mrs. See's delicious brownies and talked about their hopes for life after high school.

Now that Lottie no longer needed her as a confidant, Harriet felt free to find out what life was like outside of her small hometown.

❧

THE ORDER OF THE UNIVERSE

The first chapter of Genesis describes a step-by-step order of creation. God created matter, cycles and seasons, reproductive mechanisms.

He declared that two great lights would *rule* over the day and over the night" (verse 18).

He charged mankind to *have dominion* over every living thing that moveth upon the earth (verse 28).

The second chapter describes how God created Adam, and gave him both a home and a job in the garden of Eden (verse 15).

Then God said: "It is not good that the man should be alone; I will *make an help meet* for him" (verse 20).

He used a very special means: "And the Lord God caused a deep sleep to fall upon Adam, and he slept: and he took one of his ribs, and closed up the flesh instead thereof; And the rib, which the Lord God had taken from man, made he a woman, and brought her unto the man.

"And Adam said, This is now bone of my bones, and flesh of my flesh: she shall be called Woman, because she was taken out of Man" (verses 21-23).

God used an *orderly* process to create the universe and to prepare a place for his crowning creation: mankind, made in His own image, male and female.

In the family line that continues throughout the bible, Adam was the first man — a position of privilege and authority.

The Woman was created *to help him* in the garden, from which they could eat anything they liked, except from one forbidden tree.

Eve, although intimately connected to Adam, was given a will of her own. She used it to violate the limit.

The famous Fall.

Part of God's response to Eve's confession was "...thy desire shall be to thy husband, and *he shall rule over thee*" (Genesis 3:16).

This verse makes the command to submit to our husbands seem like punishment.

God's orderly pattern, however, laid lines of authority — and important safeguards — to cover the family.

The heavenly bodies rule over our time and our growing seasons.

Humans rule over subhuman creatures.

Husbands rule over the family — *in God's good order.*

Men and women alike have been freed from sin's curse through Christ's death on the cross.

So we wonder at New Testament instructions (see I Corinthians 11:3,

Ephesians 5: 22-24 and I Peter 3:1-6) for wives to submit to their own husbands.

We don't wonder about Ephesians 6:1: "Children, obey your parents in the Lord: for this is right." We don't view that command as a punishment.

Neither is the command to wives.

But the purpose is the same. Authority is the basis of order and protection in any social unit; for the family, for the church and its leaders, and for civil government.

The New Bible Dictionary (InterVarsity Press USA, Downers Grove, Illinois 60525, 1962) states: "...the only rightful power within creation is, ultimately, the Creator's. Such authority as men have is delegated to them by God, to whom they must answer for the way they use it. Because all authority is ultimately God's, submission to authority in all realms of life is a religious duty, part of God's service."

A husband's authority in marriage is *ordained* by God.

It is in our power, however, to strengthen those over us by voluntarily yielding our obedience and thus giving them *active* authority. An old commercial used to say, "Want him to be more of a man? Try being more of a woman."

Want him to be more of a leader? Be more of a follower.

Want him to be more of a husband?

One way to look at the authority/subject relationship is to substitute "support" for those aggravating words ("obey," "be in subjection," etc.).

Where is a foundation stone placed? At the bottom. Those in the low spots are critical to the strength of the building. A topheavy structure is unstable.

And, as you'll recall, the foundation of our spiritual house is respect for our husbands. Submission, or support, is a natural complement to genuine respect.

And if our husbands are the roofs of our spiritual houses, they can only protect us when they are over us.

Exodus 26:1-14 includes God's instructions for building a tabernacle — the elaborate tent which would serve as a place of worship for the wandering Israelites who had left Egypt.

The sides of the tabernacle were ten curtains joined together with couplings; the top consisted of *two coverings*. Verse 14 says, "And thou shalt make a covering for the tent of rams' skins dyed red, and a covering above of badgers' skins."

Our spiritual homes also have two coverings: our husband's authority, and over that, the Lord's authority.

We are well-covered when we stay underneath their protective direction.

SUBMISSION, SUBJECTION — WHY US?

Still — why do wives have to be the ones in subjection? Why can't we take turns? Why can't we just "submit to each other," as Ephesians 5:21 commands, rather than directing that women obey our husbands?

Before I gave my life to Christ, I attended a talk by one of the early feminist leaders. I came away feeling she had the answer to personal fulfillment.

The speaker convinced me that my *right* to happiness, my *right* to express myself, and my *right* to grow into a Real Person were being withheld from me by archaic traditions.

And here was a ray of hope, a movement to liberate women from You Know Who's domination.

The speaker graciously assured us the movement would be a good thing for men, too, to free them from "the worries and stresses attendant to breadwinning." We would share the load (provided we got commensurate salaries).

A win-win proposition!

But a year later I committed my life to Jesus Christ and began to study the bible. The more I learned of God's plan for His female creatures, the more clearly I saw how opposed is the direction of the world to entice women away from the home and their traditional roles, and to direct their energies and affections to temporal, selfish, unfeminine pursuits.

Looking back on those past decades, what has the women's liberation movement brought us?

Big gains in women's pay and opportunities for promotion. This certainly seems just and reasonable for women who have to work, and there are many who do.

Women feel they are making a greater contribution to society at large than by merely raising children and doing housework — although women may of course choose to be housewives.

So, isn't everybody happy now?

Well — for a start, the funds to raise women's salaries, provide re-entry vocational training for women, provide child-care centers for working mothers, provide free birth-control supplies, abortion clinics and other adjustments to equalize the sexes come right out of the pockets of every consumer and taxpayer.

A family trying to live on one salary is at a financial disadvantage to a two-income family. The choice to be "just a housewife" is an increasingly costly one.

Surely limiting the income per family hinders the market for wasteful nonsense like electric tie racks, and thus slows consumption of our dwindling resources?

(No, the copyright date is the same as the last time you checked!)

What about the impact of an expanded female job force on commute traffic and gasoline supply? How much material excess is purchased by working wives who have "earned a few luxuries"? How many family men are jobless because women have preferential status in hiring guidelines?

And why have women *chosen* the "worries and stress attendant to breadwinning" from which they claimed men needed relief?

The moral double-standard was also a target. No longer would women be treated as sex objects preyed upon by men. Now women can do the preying, can hook up with whatever man catches one's fancy rather than honoring sex as the physical expression of an emotional and legal commitment — or to recognize its place in God's design: a unique blessing for righteously-joined men and women.

Perhaps the most serious harm resulting from this movement is devaluation of the role of parenthood. Illegitimacy is no longer a source of shame, but a deliberate choice made by those who want children but not marriage. Abortion is among the options for those who want sex but not children.

The traditional responsibilities of motherhood — to nurture, to civilize, to teach life skills and moral values — are readily abandoned to the educational system, to a worn-out grandparent, or to a childcare provider (often one who turns in the lowest bid — why are champions of women's rights willing to exploit other women?).

That the movement elicits at least a little agreement from almost all women, and its proponents sincerely believe their aims are *good* brings to mind the scriptural warning: "...Satan himself is transformed into an angel of light" (II Corinthians 11:14).

Our culture has been blinded by this deceptive light.

Sadly, missionary wife, other women may condemn you more for submitting to your husband than for divorcing him.

Romans 12:2 reads, "And be not conformed to this world, but be ye transformed by the renewing of your mind, that ye may prove what is that good, and acceptable, and perfect will of God."

It was God's sovereign choice — His good, and acceptable, and perfect will — to establish family order.

Now, while blind obedience is better than disobedience, we like to have rationale. God understands that. When we ask for wisdom, God will graciously give it — if we ask in faith, not in resistance.

So here are some good things that result when we follow His directions for marital order:

- A husband can make decisions with confidence that his wife will support him and will do her part to carry them out. Effective obedience means not merely doing as we're told, but being loyal and trustworthy. "The heart of her husband doth safely trust in her..." according to Proverbs 31:11.

She will neither ridicule her husband's ideas, nor will she (not in her husband's presence, anyway!) fall to her knees and ask God to forestall the disaster she expects.

Whatever her misgivings, she allows her husband to learn from experience. If he fails, she comforts him and expresses confidence that he will recoup the loss. If he succeeds, she congratulates him (and privately thanks God she didn't voice her negative opinion beforehand).

This provides valuable exercise for a husband to grow in leadership skills.

- The obedient wife manifests the spiritual fruit of faithfulness by carrying out her husband's requests with cheerful efficiency.
- Remember that your husband is the roof of your spiritual house. A roof only protects when it is above you.

Practically speaking, subjection bestows authority on those who have responsibilities toward us: our husbands, our spiritual leaders, our government, our Lord.

While we can't thwart the ultimate aims of our Lord with our disobedience, we do forfeit His blessings. Our rebellion certainly can thwart a husband's plans, hinder our church's testimony, and damage social order.

- We strengthen our own faith by obeying in spite of our preferences because God commanded it. He doesn't have to command us to do what we would naturally do.
- Being in subjection to another human is a terrific character exercise which can dislodge pride, contentiousness, arrogance and other ungodly traits.
- Stress is an equal-opportunity health problem for men and women. Why not release burdens that were not designed for you, and make it easier for your husband to carry them by replacing your opposition with support?

  You will both benefit.
- Our call is to submit to our husbands as unto the Lord. Andrew Murray describes a "perfect rest" available to wholehearted disciples by: "Giving up one's whole life to him, for Him alone to rule and order it; taking up His yoke, and submitting to be led and taught, to learn of Him; abiding to be and do only what He wills —" (*Abide in Christ*, Barbour and Company, Inc., Ulrichsville, Ohio 44683, 1992.)

A wife's submission to her husband covers much of "what He wills" for her.

'STOP LEADING!'

When I was in junior high, I was taller than all the other girls and most of the boys in my class. It was a huge detriment, at that gawky stage of life.

My ninth-grade physical education teacher, preparing us for a more promising social future, made my misery complete by teaching us ballroom dancing.

You guessed it. There weren't enough boys in the class to match up with all the girls, so the teacher gave me a sex-change designation. I had to dance with another girl.

I learned the leading steps to all the dances. Eventually I got to be pretty good at pointing our arms where we were heading and pushing my partner forward.

When I was old enough to go to a dance with a boy, everything was backwards from what I had learned. My escort finally yelled at me: "Stop leading!"

Marriage is like dancing — lovely when its complementary roles — leader and follower — work together. Otherwise, it's full of stumbles.

DO WE HAVE TO SUBMIT TO ALL MEN?

No!

Ephesians 5:22 and I Peter 3:1 both specify that we are to submit to our own husbands — not to all men.

Women have many opportunities to exercise leadership in life. In fact, biblical examples of "leading women" include Lydia, the businesswoman; Deborah, the judge; the queen of Sheba.

We can hold managerial or executive positions in the workplace; we can hold offices in civic, social, charitable, or church groups. We can run for president.

In fact, scripture instructs us to lead our children and to teach younger women.

Outside the home, our leadership is self-regulating. If we do a poor job, we are demoted, voted out, or dropped from a mentoring relationship.

In the home, however, the family goes into dysfunction when leadership fails — or when our "followership" fails.

In a business or a community association, roles are arrayed in "reporting relationships" — who is accountable to whom — or an organizational chart, which displays the flow of authority.

That is the essence of what scripture has provided for us in the home: the husband accountable to Christ, the wife accountable to the husband, and the children accountable to both parents (see Ephesians 5:23 and 6:1-4).

Yes, the husband is accountable to Christ, even if he is not yet a believer. God delegates authority, and husbands must answer to Him for their use of it — another good reason for us to help, not hinder, our mates.

It is "worldly wisdom" that has quarreled with this divine order by exalting women's rights and children's rights and blurring gender distinctions.

FOLLOW THE MODEL: 'INDIGENIZATION'

When I embraced Christianity, my value-system took such a jolt that I wanted to change my life entirely — including my marital life. I tried to impose my new standards on my husband. This was a serious mistake.

Natural talents and material concerns *do* deserve a low priority in *my* life, but these things are the *substance* of my husband's life.

Missionaries going to a foreign culture are taught the importance of indigenization — of submitting to the cultural norms. They are sent to proclaim the Gospel of Jesus Christ, not to Americanize the nationals.

Household missionaries also have to respect the culture of the man we want to win — our job is to give our husbands the experience of godly love and the challenging example of a life lived for Christ, not to force them into a new mode of external behavior.

Yes, ultimately we want our men to value spiritual pursuits above hobbies, vocation, and secular knowledge — but it has to be their personal, voluntary decision. Scoffing at the importance they place on temporal things only causes resentment, hurt, and a breakdown in personal communications.

TYING OUR TWO LOVES TOGETHER

The exhortation to submit to our husbands *as to the Lord* gives us some good guidelines:

For example, we're commanded to praise the Lord. Nowhere are we invited to find fault with Him! What do you praise the Lord for? For His creation, His actions, His answers to prayer, His provision of your needs, His character, His love.

So should our appreciation be toward our husbands: comprehensive recognition of all they do for us, all the praiseworthy elements of their characters and personalities.

Second, we're told to *give thanks in everything,* to make our requests known *with thanksgiving.*

We definitely should express our needs and our desires to our husbands — as we do in our prayers — and remember to thank them for fulfillment.

Yet, even the Lord says "no" to many of our requests.

Our husbands need to know they can say "no" without fear of a cold shoulder, of wheedling, pleading, and arguments, which only stiffen his resolve, or, worse, drive him to give in and abdicate his authority.

Rather, we share Paul's experience in learning how to be abased as well as how to abound. We learn to be contentedly grateful in every circumstance.

An attitude tuned toward wisdom and understanding can yield instruction from a husband's "no's." Asking a man to declare his goals and expectations can be threatening to him, but a wife can discern her husband's will by observing the limits he imposes.

TAKE HIS NAME

Jesus has given us a no-holds-barred commitment of His love by allowing us to act "in His name."

And a husband shares his reputation, his credit — all that he is — by giving his name to his wife.

Worldy wisdom, however, proposes that couples soft-pedal their commitment to each other. A modified wedding vow is to stay together "as long as we both shall *love*."

Side by side with that conditional promise is a woman's rejection of name change. It is trendy for a bride to "protect her own identity" or "make a name for herself" by retaining her own surname — possibly appending her husband's name to hers with a hyphen.

This diminishes the bride's investment in the marriage.

If you recall, one of the goals of the tower builders at Babel was "to make us a name" (Genesis 11:4). The result was confusion of languages and dispersion.

You only need look at the offspring of two-surname parents to see confusion.

Take your husband's name and wear it proudly. Bring honor upon it in all that you do.

We call ourselves Christians because we are one with Christ. Calling ourselves "Mrs. Husband" denotes that we are one with him.

THE SECOND 'S' — SACRIFICE

Christ laid down his life for us.

And He said, "Greater love hath no man than this, that a man lay down his life for his friends" (John 15:13).

Laying down our lives is the ultimate obedience to His two great commandments: to love God with all that is in us and to love our husbands as we love ourselves.

How do we do this in our marriages?

HONOR HIS PRIORITIES

Leadership is again the issue (or battle!) as we compete with our husbands about how to spend money or leisure time, whether to buy a new car or a new sofa, whether to give the kids music lessons or send them to sports camp.

Our son, we feel, is musically gifted — something special, while everybody plays soccer! The best thing for our boy would be piano lessons. But your husband is adamant that physical activity is the right choice.

Sometimes a wife's career is threatening to a husband. The obvious *sacrifice* may be for her to allow her husband to be the family provider.

On the other hand, Willa's husband wanted her to continue her career after they married so she would secure a retirement income of her own.

God is the Overseer of all our issues of conflict. Romans 12:18 advises: "If it be possible, as much as lieth in you, live peaceably with all men."

Take a step of faith and yield to your husband. Trust God to bring about the best for you and your family through your husband's decisions — or to change them in a mutually-satisfactory way. Obeying him is, in most cases, obeying Him.

Meanwhile, each sacrifice you make is a "death to self" that refines your character and beautifies the hidden man of the heart.

ADOPT HIS INTERESTS AS YOUR OWN

Another sacrifice we can make is to "take an interest in his interests."

Obviously we exclude unrighteous activities, but there is a whole realm of shared hobbies we can participate in to increase friendship, companionship, admiration — all constructive materials for a sound home.

We reject him by being dismissive of the ways he likes to spend his free time.

Yes, our heart's longing is for him to share *our* interests in Christ and in the work of the church, but for now — see how God will bless your sacrifice.

Do unto him *as you would like him to do* unto you.

THE THIRD 'S' — SUFFERING

There's suffering and there's suffering in a marriage.

Suffering for righteousness' sake glorifies God, beautifies our character, and builds our heavenly reward. Putting up with our husbands' belittling of our faith, his in-your-face bad habits, his unnecessarily coarse language, his waste of time and family resources are opportunities for us to "let patience have her perfect(ing) work" in us.

There is some suffering we need to reject, however. When a man physically abuses us or our children, it's timeout time.

Sometimes the only scripture an abusive husband knows is the one directed to women: submit to your own husband.

The ones he doesn't know are directed to him: to love his wife as Christ loves the church — to give himself for her, as Christ did for the church.

Ephesians 5:28-29 says "so ought men to love their wives as their own bodies. He that loveth his wife loveth himself. *For no man ever yet hated his own flesh; but nourisheth and cherisheth it*, even as the Lord the church."

When a man is destructive against a woman's flesh, he is way out of order. Immediately seek pastoral counsel, and go to the agency or shelter he recommends. Put yourself under a *protective* authority, which may include police involvement and legal measures. Trust the experience of others, rather than your vacillating emotions.

Then there is suffering apart from what we experience in marriage — ill health, financial loss, unfairness in the workplace, mean neighbors — the everyday woes of living in a fallen world.

Our good friend Peter tells us (I Peter 4:12-14) " Beloved, think it not strange concerning the fiery trial which is to try you, as though some strange thing happened unto you:

"But rejoice, inasmuch as ye are partakers of Christ's sufferings; that, when his glory shall be revealed, ye may be glad also with exceeding joy.

"If ye be reproached for the name of Christ, happy are ye; for the spirit of glory and of God resteth upon you: on their part he is evil spoken of, but on your part he is glorified."

We are not exempt from the "fiery trials" that afflict mortals.

And we must never expect or proclaim that life is a bed of roses for a Christian — trials are part of God's plan — to produce His glory and our joy! (Re-read James 1:2-4.)

How we respond to our trials is our opportunity to shine the courage and character of Christ about us.

My friend Lynn was diagnosed with terminal cancer when she was only fifty years old, with a teenager still at home.

She bravely endured gruesome treatments which were only going to buy her time, not healing.

But she determined she would live each of her remaining days to the glory of God, to spend her remaining energy in his service.

Her last work was to start a home bible study in her neighborhood — on the book of James. I was one of her students.

As the inevitable end came, we met around her hospital bed, then her hospice bed. Lynn fought the good fight. She finished the course. She taught her bible study group, her family, her friends how to live — and how to die — to the glory of God.

SUFFERING IS THE BASIS OF GRACE

God's grace toward us was not a shrug of His shoulders as He decided to overlook a sin — His grace was Christ bearing a rough, heavy cross on His shoulders to His place of crucifixion.

Grace always costs something to the one who is offended.

We extend grace by bearing the cost; suffering a hurt, or a loss, without retaliation or endless recrimination.

We grow in grace through enduring an unpleasant situation rather than making our own "way of escape."

Suffering gracefully beautifies the "hidden man of the heart (with) the ornament of a meek and quiet spirit, which is in the sight of God of great price" (I Peter 3:4).

SELF-INDUCED SUFFERING

Peter contrasts the suffering that glorifies God with the suffering we bring upon ourselves. "For what glory is it, if, when ye be buffeted *for your faults*, ye shall take it patiently? but if, when ye do well, and suffer for it, ye take it patiently, this is acceptable with God.

"for even hereunto were ye called: because Christ also suffered for us, leaving us an example, that ye should follow his steps:

"Who did no sin, neither was guile found in his mouth:

"Who, *when he was reviled, reviled not again; when he suffered, he threatened not*; but committed himself to him that judgeth righteously" (I Peter 2:20-23, emphasis added).

Since suffering is plentiful in this life, why not eliminate the suffering that we bring on our own heads? It doesn't glorify God, so it is devoid of purpose.

What are some examples?

IRRESPONSIBILITY. Has the electricity been cut off because you forgot to pay the bill? The car broke down because you forgot to check the oil or water?

UNDISCIPLINE. Are you prone to chronic lateness? Making promises without taking steps to fulfill them? Spending first and balancing the checkbook later?

MANIPULATION. Do you put your husband on the spot when you want him to do something so it's difficult for him to refuse? Try to make him feel guilty or ashamed? Bargain with him for sexual favors? Enlist your children or his mother in your campaigns to counter his plans?

CONTENTIOUSNESS. Nagging, sarcasm, negativity. Being easily offended. Deliberately misunderstanding to put someone else in the wrong; wearing a chip on your shoulder; looking for slights in every conversation.

DISOBEDIENCE (duh!). I expect my husband to provide my needs. If he tells me not to spend any more money this month, but I come across an irresistible sale and spend $75, even if I get $200 worth of clothes and believe I'm "doing him good," I have spoiled his plans for that money.

Perhaps he wanted to save for my Christmas present! Or he may have noted, but neglected to mention, that the property tax bill is due. He cannot fully meet his responsibilities without my *cooperation*, which is another word for wifely submissiveness.

All these *character problems* are likely to cause fireworks and retaliation from our husbands.

If it seems like we bear an unfair burden in keeping our marriages harmonious, look at the root problem — character. Character, the very thing God wants to perfect in *us*, his children.

So remove the hindrances to His work, and ease the unnecessary suffering. We are always winners when we do things God's way.

SUFFERING THROUGH DISAPPOINTMENTS

Another type of self-induced suffering is: setting unrealistic expectations. It's a sure-fire prescription for disappointment.

With our husbands, our wrong expectations usually come from poor communication (on his part) or from presumption (on our part). Before you take offense at something you thought he was or was not going to do, review whether you misunderstood what he promised, whether you took an off-hand comment as a promise, or whether "he ought to know that when you asked for A you also wanted B."

We can also suffer unnecessarily in our church life — or lack thereof. Like Harriet, we can invest time and affection in church to the neglect of home life and impoverish our marriages. Or we can overemphasize the amount of church attendance *we feel we need*, and wallow in self-pity.

Review chapter 4, and see whether some of the activities you're missing are essential or merely desirable. Are they worth fighting over — or suffering over?

SUFFERING AS AN UNEQUALLY-YOKED WIFE

If you married in disobedience, or otherwise feel like your unequal marriage is "self-induced suffering," please re-read the segment, "Removing Hindrances is Necessary Preparation for Household Ministry" in Chapter 2.

God has forgiven you. He will use your marriage for good purposes in your life and in others'.

BUD'S STORY: A NEW WOMAN IN HIS LIFE

Bud had a new idea for a business of his own, and it was — eventually — a winner.

With Lottie involved as his secretary and bookkeeper, and their elder son as right-hand man, they began to prosper.

Bud bought an airplane.

Both their sons and their youngest daughter took flying lessons. Family camping took a backseat to family flying, and the local pilots formed the family's new social circle.

One of Bud's favorite new friends was a gentle, white-haired lady who flew a pink-and-silver airplane.

Mrs. See.

She was more than twenty years older than Bud, every inch a lady, every inch a follower of Jesus Christ.

Bud was only one of her airport fans. All his fellow pilots adopted her, vying for the privilege to help her with mechanical problems or decisions about upgrades or maintenance routines.

She took a special liking to Bud, though. His daughter, Harriet, had been one of "her girls" in the junior women's circle she sponsored at church.

She became a lifelong friend. Bud would eventually help sell her little plane when age and declining health grounded her. He would eventually chauffeur her to doctor appointments when Mrs. See's vision and driver's license also lapsed.

Bud was a different man in her presence, cleaning up his language, hiding his usual impatience with his family, on his best behavior, responding to the godly spirit of Mrs. See.

EXERCISE 1
BIBLE STUDY:
GOD'S PURPOSES FOR SUBMISSION

1. Read Romans 13:1-5. Who ordains "powers" and establishes rulers (authorities)? For what purpose?

2. Read John 19:10-11. Whose will did Pilate fulfill by using his power to crucify Jesus?

3. Read Proverbs 8:15 and Proverbs 21:1. Who is ultimately ruling over our world?

4. Read I Corinthians 11:3. Diagram the flow of authority from God to woman:

- GOD
-
-
- WOMAN

5. Read Hebrews 13:17. How is a woman's submission to her husband beneficial to her?

6. CONSIDER:

- What would your nation, state, or city be like if there were no authority structure to oversee its operations?

- What would the military forces be like without a "chain of command"?

- What would family life be like if there were no expectation that children would be subject to their parents' authority?

- How is a wife's willingness to conform to her authority roles (under her husband, over her children) beneficial to the operation of her family?

EXERCISE 2
LEARN FROM YOUR LIMITS

Being an unequally-yoked Christian wife may prevent us from participating in such church-sponsored events as family camp, sweetheart banquets, week-long revivals,

____

____

______________________________(fill in your own examples).

Are we the only individuals who encounter exclusion to such activities? Who else is unlikely to attend?

What purpose does God have in allowing limitation? (See Acts 16:6-7)

Was Paul's work for God diminished because he didn't get to go to these places (See Acts 19:1-12)?

Are we going to miss out on some good things because of our present limits? (See Joel 2:23-27, Psalm 37:3-5, and Psalm 138:8)

We may be privileged to suffer persecution for Christ's sake, both at home and at church. What are some instances where you have experienced ill-treatment at either place?

At home (example: ridicule of beliefs)	At church (example: judgmentalism)
•	•
•	•
•	•
•	•
•	•

Which complaints can you redefine as examples of Christ's sufferings?

EXERCISE 3
LOOK ON THE FIELD:
HOW CAN I BE A VALUABLE HELPER TO MY HUSBAND?

In his career:

- take an interest in what he does
- applaud his victories at work
- help him with wardrobe selection and care (laundry, dry cleaning, mending)
-
-

Family health:

- purchase and prepare nutritious foods for meals and snacks
- plan and participate in family games and physical activities
-
-

Family possessions:

- judicious selection
- faithful maintenance
-
-

Children:

- Encourage good character qualities
- Oversee homework and assigned household chores
- Teach life skills
-

EXERCISE 4
LOOK ON THE FIELD:
WHAT ARE YOUR HUSBAND'S INTERESTS?

Philippians 2:4 - Look not every man on his own things, but every man also on the things of others.

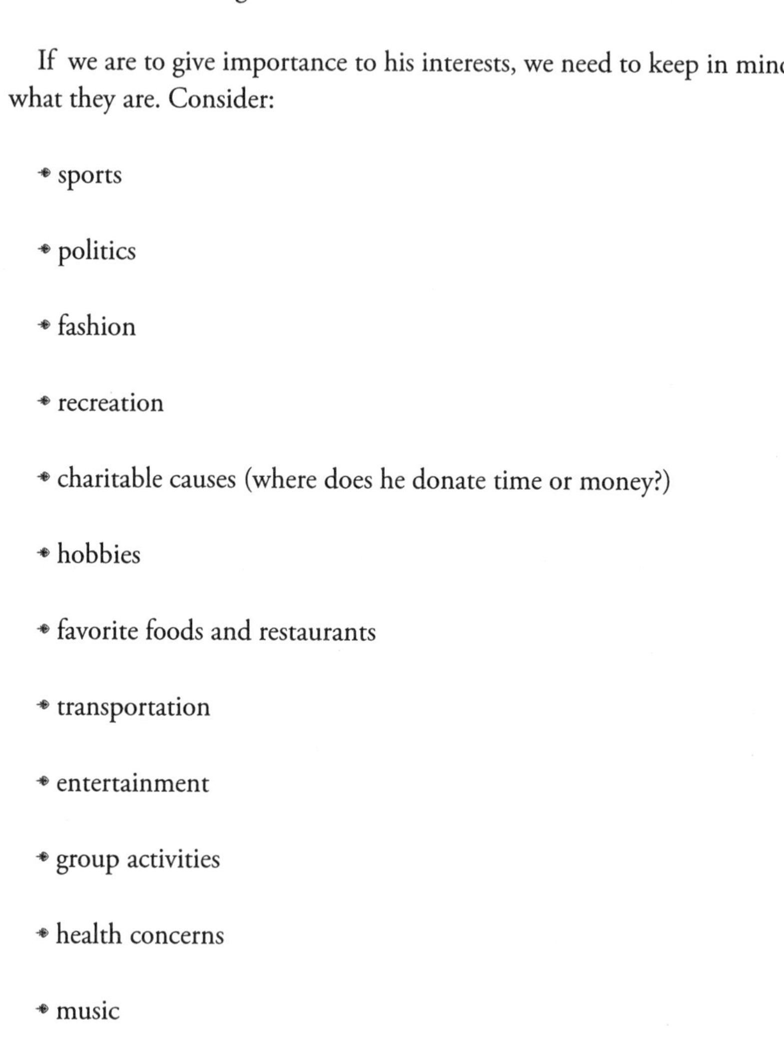

If we are to give importance to his interests, we need to keep in mind what they are. Consider:

- sports
- politics
- fashion
- recreation
- charitable causes (where does he donate time or money?)
- hobbies
- favorite foods and restaurants
- transportation
- entertainment
- group activities
- health concerns
- music
- books, reading material

EXERCISE 5
OFFER A SACRIFICE OF THANKSGIVING

What things aggravate you about your husband's behavior or character (in other words, if complaining were allowed, what would go on this list)?

Behavior:

-
-
-
-

Character:

-
-
-
-

Now: go through the list and, as an act of sacrifice, thank God for each item. Then ask yourself: what divine purpose could be served IN MY LIFE by my husband's "faults"?

Stimulating fault

-
-
-
-
-

Corresponding purpose

-
-
-
-
-

EXERCISE 6
FAULTS MAY POINT TO NEEDS

Review your list in the previous exercise. Now consider each trait with a view to how he may be responding to a need in his life. For example, living beyond his means may be a bid for the approval of others, stinginess may be a need for security, etc.

Try to understand your man by discerning what makes him act as he does.

Trait	Expression of need for:
◆	
◆	
◆	
◆	
◆	
◆	
◆	
◆	
◆	

Then intercede for him, asking the Father to meet his underlying need and to show you ways you can be part of that answer.

CHAPTER 7

"Show, Don't Tell"

The Neglected Demonstration

BUD'S STORY: FACING SURGERY

Harriet had come from California for a short visit to her parents.

When it was time for her return flight, Bud and Lottie took her to the airport. As they walked down the long corridor toward her departure gate, Bud suddenly stopped and sat in the nearest chair.

Harriet and Lottie both went white and stooped over him. "What's wrong?" Lottie asked.

Bud shook his head impatiently. "My legs just gave out on me," he said.

In a few minutes he got up and resumed his walk with them. But he had to stop once more before they reached the gate.

During the next months he underwent numerous tests to look for the cause of his leg problem, which intensified until he could hardly walk. Finally, an orthopedist determined he had a pinched nerve in his spine. Surgery was indicated.

No one except Bud liked the prospect of spinal surgery. But Bud was very optimistic and excited. As soon as he got out of the hospital, everything would be like it used to be.

∞

FOLLOWING PAUL'S PRINCIPLES?

No less an evangelist than Saint Paul wrote in I Corinthians 2:1-5:

"And I, Brethren, when I came to you, came not with excellency of speech or of wisdom, declaring unto you the testimony of God.

"For I determined not to know any thing among you, save Jesus Christ, and him crucified.

"And I was with you in weakness, and in fear, and in much trembling.

"And my speech and my preaching was not with enticing words of man's wisdom, but in *demonstration of the Spirit and of power:*

"That your faith should not stand in the wisdom of men, but in the power of God" (emphasis added).

Even without the constraint to win converts "without a word," Paul relied on demonstration of the Spirit and of power, not argument — the "enticing words of man's wisdom."

How can we invoke those same instruments — demonstration of the Spirit, and power — to entice our husbands toward faith in Christ? How do we "show 'em what we've got?"

We have three assets to put on display:

- the evidence of our changing lives, as we grow into the likeness of our Savior
- the powers that develop in us as we grow closer to our Savior, and
- our performance of the works that God has appointed for us to do.

A CHANGING LIFE: THE IMPORTANCE OF ABIDING IN CHRIST

In earlier chapters, we looked at construction of the earthly homes we share with our husbands.

The home we make for the Lord Jesus Christ calls for some of the same attitudes:

- SUBMISSION - to His will, spelled out in His Word
- SACRIFICE - taking up our cross daily, where we crucify our worldly passions, our pride and self-concerns, and
- SUFFERING - as we take our stand for righteousness, and when we undergo the perfecting work of patience under trial.

Through Him, with Him, because of Him, we endure the disapproval and opposition of a hedonistic, self-exalting culture.

Trusting Him, we joyfully greet the trials that transform and deepen our character into His chaste, gentle, quiet, confident likeness.

When our submission produces support, cooperation, loyalty and dependability to our husbands, we express our support, cooperation, loyalty and dependability to the Lord Jesus Christ.

The trust we place in our husbands' decisions reflects our trust in the Lord's care and protection of us.

Think about it this way: split-screen television — two faces side-by-side in the viewing window — gives us an analogy of how it works to submit to our husbands "as unto the Lord."

When your husband asks you to do something, imagine the Lord Jesus sharing a "split screen" with him, confirming the request.

When we comply, the Lord approves and applauds along with our mates.

Jesus has told us in His word how to develop a supportive relationship that will cause our husbands to "sit up and take notice."

HOSPITALITY OF THE HEART

As for that other home, our challenge as Jesus' hostesses is to make Him comfortable in our hearts:

- to give Him a place of rest within our "quiet spirits"
- to nourish Him with our praises and gratitude
- to fellowship with Him in ongoing prayer
- to rejoice in Him — to delight in our Lord!

Robert Boyd Munger wrote a booklet called *My Heart — Christ's Home* (InterVarsity Press, Downers Grove, IL 60515-1426, revised edition ©1986) which has become a classic depiction of what happens — and needs to happen — when Christ takes up residence in a human heart.

I recommend that you add a copy to your devotional library, and read it often. It provides a charming inventory of what a house guest might find when a believer lets Him explore beyond the entryway.

The greater freedom Christ has in our interior life, the brighter His light will shine in us.

And as we delight in Him, beholding His glory, II Corinthians 3:18 says we "are changed into the same image from glory to glory, even as by the Spirit of the Lord."

THE IMPORTANCE OF A HEALTHY 'SELF-LOVE'

Jesus' second great commandment is for us to "love our neighbor *as we love ourselves*" (emphasis added).

Loving ourselves is a difficult concept, because "self" is the source of many of our spiritual problems. We are very suspicious of "self."

Through the Holy Spirit, we grow in the spiritual fruit of *self-control,* which includes denying self, and "dying to self" — setting aside selfish priorities and ambitions which spring from *self-will.* Self-will, the source of rebellion and pride, is always a competitor for God's will.

Other elements we need to recognize and rein are:

- SELF-DISPARAGEMENT - dwelling on your faults, inabilities, and your evil history. This doesn't make you humble — it makes you discouraged, unproductive and joyless.

Apply Philippians 4:8 to yourself once in a while: "Finally, brethren, whatsoever things are true, whatsoever things are honest, whatsoever things are just, whatsoever things are pure, whatsoever things are lovely, whatsoever things are of good report; if there by any virtue, and if there be any praise, think on these things."

- SELF-CONDEMNATION - looking back at the messes you've made and the consequences that continue. They are facts of your life — but your life belongs to God.

Paul offers his example in Philippians 3:13: "...forgetting those things which are behind, and reaching forth unto those things which are before, I press toward the mark for the prize of the high calling of God in Christ Jesus."

Look *forward* at the wonders in store as you participate in God's program for you.

- SELF-PROTECTION - resisting criticism, refusing risky assignments, opposing change — even beneficial change. Sometimes that famous "comfort zone" we are accused of staying in isn't comfortable at all — it's just familiar.

To benefit from this "trial laboratory" we live in, make a daily commitment to allow the Lord to change you.

- SELF-IMPOSED PRESSURE - to be the perfect wife/mother/daughter-in-law/ ___________(you fill in the blank); to outperform a rival in the workplace (or in the church?), setting unrealistic deadlines or quotas for youself. Our unrest comes from struggling to meet standards that God hasn't set for us.
- SELF-PITY - is practically the hallmark of unequally-yoked wives. I'll be the first to agree that we have grounds.

If we look at our situation with our "natural eyes," we are constantly torn between our two worlds: our yearning to express our faith freely in the company of fellow believers, and the *rightful* expectations of a very secular husband.

But self-pity can turn into an idol. By letting self-pity rule, we can excuse ourselves from walking in God's ways. It's a very seductive force which can steal away our inner joy and peace, and turn our love for our husbands to resentment.

Looking at our life from a heavenly point of view, however, from "where we are seated with Christ" (see Ephesians 2:6), we are privileged to be a potential bridge between our Savior and that very secular husband.

Whenever your self-pity is stimulated by a put-down from a church-goer, or a nasty comment from your husband, or just by the day-after-day sameness of your life — reject the temptation to feel sorry for yourself.

Consider such "downers" to be a tiny share of suffering with Christ. He endured abuse and misunderstandings — and He is well-acquainted with waiting for people to respond to His love. (How long did He wait for you?)

The "self" we need to treat with healthy regard is who we are as a unique creation of God. *Self-worth* is the blessing we are to hold onto to love ourselves rightly.

We must love ourselves *wisely* in order to love others well.

We are not to *indulge* ourselves — making excuses for our bad behavior or omissions, or compensating ourselves for disappointments by eating a half-dozen doughnuts or otherwise gratifying a sensual appetite — just as *indulgence* is not a healthy way to love other people.

Neither are we to *loathe* ourselves. We are to rejoice in what God has given us in talent, skill, intelligence, health — He put a lot of care into our construction. Read Psalm 139 for a great dose of self-worth.

Chances are, your sense of self-worth has been battered in the past.

That was then. Now God has declared us accepted in Christ. We are taught and nourished and empowered by the Holy Spirit. We are adopted as His daughters!

In Matthew 10:29-31, Jesus describes how God values us:

"Are not two sparrows sold for a farthing? and one of them shall not fall on the ground without your Father.

"But the very hairs of your head are all numbered.

"Fear ye not therefore, ye are of more value than many sparrows."

Think of that everytime you wipe your fallen hairs off the bathroom counter.

PUTTING THE PIECES TOGETHER

To reclaim what God intended, we need a *unified* self:

- AN UNDIVIDED HEART - with our affections set on the things God loves, not the things of the world. Psalm 86:11-12 says, "Teach me thy way, O Lord; I will walk in thy truth: *unite my heart* to fear thy name.

"I will praise thee, O Lord my God, *with all my heart:* and I will glorify thy name for evermore."

- AN UNDIVIDED MIND - the agent of change where the Holy Spirit transforms us. James 1:8 says, "A double minded man is unstable in all his ways."

He gives his remedy in James 4:8: "Draw nigh to God, and he will draw nigh to you. Cleanse your hands, ye sinners, and purify your hearts, ye double minded."

- AN UNDIVIDED PURPOSE - devoted to doing things — all things — God's way. The result will be a life of consistency and integrity.

Psalm 139:23-24 provides this excellent prayer:

"Search me, O God, and know my heart; try me, and know my thoughts:

"And see if there be any wicked way in me, and lead me in the way everlasting."

We need to live a life *separated to God.*

II Corinthians 6:17-7:1 says, "Wherefore come out from among them, and *be ye separate*, saith the Lord, and touch not the unclean thing, and I will receive you,

"And will be a Father unto you, and ye shall be my sons and daughters, said the Lord Almighty.

"Having therefore these promises, dearly beloved, let us cleanse ourselves from all filthiness of the flesh and spirit, perfecting holiness in the fear of God."

SPIRITUAL SELF-CARE

Our responsibilities to ourselves are

- to grow in godly wisdom
- to study "to show ourselves approved unto God, rightly dividing the Word"
- to keep an open channel of communication with Him through prayer
- to confess and turn from known sin
- to release our cares to Him
- to live a life of gratitude, and
- to cultivate contentment in all circumstances.

You are the only one who can do these things for yourself.

CLEAN YOUR HANDS!

A particular responsibility is to see to the "cleanness of our hands."

Remember the description of the woman who either builds her house — or tears it down *with her own hands*?

Be diligent to identify your "deeds of demolition" every day: the hurtful words, belittling remarks, deliberate misunderstandings, refusal to meet a request, obstinacy....

Confess them to God, and appeal to Him for restoration.

This is a particularly good prelude to a prayer of intercession for our husbands. Psalm 24:3-4 says, "Who shall ascend into the hill of the Lord? or who shall stand in his holy place?

"He that hath *clean hands*, and a pure heart; who hath not lifted up his soul unto vanity, nor sworn deceitfully."

CLEANING YOUR INNER HOUSE

Two relationship-damaging hindrances are common to women in spiritually-divided homes: anger and bitterness. They are antithetical to the "ornament of a meek and quiet spirit, which is in the sight of God of great price."

GIVE ANGER A CURFEW

Ephesians 4: 26-27 warns: "Be ye angry, and sin not: let not the sun go down upon your wrath: Neither give place to the devil."

We live in a world which will inspire us to anger many times a day — and most of us live with a husband who can do the same thing for us.

Anger is a valid emotion. Some of it is righteous anger — furious indignation against societal sins, blasphemous speech, mockery of things we hold sacred.

The devil is ever alert for our hot spots of anger, and seizes any opportunity to provoke us into words of condemnation, loss of self-control, or retaliatory action.

Instead, discharge your anger in prayer, counting it privilege to share in Christ's suffering over this sorry world. Then turn over your volatile emotion to Him.

"Vengeance is mine," He said. "I will repay" (Romans 12:19).

Trust Him to take care of all that is wrong, and let Him reign as Prince of Peace in your heart.

Sometimes our anger is ego-activated when we have been thwarted, disrespected, inadvertently or deliberately offended.

Talk to the Lord about it, acknowledging that He has allowed the humbling experience to take place.

Identify what has to go to restore your peace, and turn the energy of your anger against it: your pride, your greed, your worldly ambition — whatever got jarred — and refuse to give the offense any room in your heart.

If you entered into a verbal exchange with the person who wounded you, make amends quickly.

In the marital relationship, it is a good idea to study your anger. What exactly pushes your "hot button?" The devil knows your vulnerable spots. Your husband knows them. You ought to know them, too.

If unforgiveness, resentment, or shame is the kindling that sparks your anger — pray your way to freedom.

If it's overreaction because you have never tamed your tendency to flare up over every little offense — do it now.

"Get wisdom and understanding." Do you share some blame for the incident? Are there mitigating circumstances in the other person's favor? Is there an old problem you need to confront, and either give or invite apology?

Many married couples claim their secret of marital harmony is "never go to bed mad." Good plan.

Another good plan is to prepare an "arsenal of blessings" so you can respond proactively when your mate makes you angry. Paul said in Romans 12:21, "Be not overcome with evil, but overcome evil with good."

I Peter 3:9 repeats the principle: "Not rendering evil for evil, or railing for railing: but contrariwise blessing; know that ye are thereunto called, that ye should inherit a blessing."

It is hard to think of a blessing to offer in the heat of an angry moment, so plan ahead.

For example, use your anger-energy to prepare a little treat for him — microwave popcorn or cinnamon toast.

Wash his car windows.

Do one of his chores.

Rub — or kiss — his neck (when you want to wring it).

Think of little tokens of "goodness" you can turn your attention to when Satan would like you to lose control.

A simple blessing is to be the first to say, "I'm sorry."

If your husband is hiding out after your spat, and you can't minister a good deed directly to him, use your energy to clean a closet or cupboard, tackle the mending pile or the ironing basket, or walk around the block (as many times as it takes to dissipate your ire).

While you work — or walk — invite the Prince of Peace to develop in you that quiet spirit which is of great price in God's sight.

He is a willing teacher. He tells us in Matthew 11:29: "Take my yoke upon you, and learn of me: for I am meek and lowly in heart: and ye shall find rest unto your souls."

BEWARE OF BURIED ROOTS

Unresolved anger and unforgiven offenses are rich garden soil in which a "root of bitterness" may spring up (see Hebrews 12:15), and affect many other people — particularly your family.

Other sources of bitterness include:

- broken promises
- unfulfilled expectations
- jealousy
- betrayal.

Anything we bury deep in the dark corners of our hearts will begin to grow roots and bear bitter fruit.

The remedy is the grace of God — always abundantly available to the believer. Submit your wounds to the Savior, who has already experienced every evil the world can invent.

Decide now, and renew your decision frequently, that every offense you encounter will take you straight to the throne of grace, to His Light.

Like washing dishes and dusting furniture in our temporal homes, we need to give daily attention to spiritual cleansing.

WHEN YOU NEED DEEPER CLEANING

Condemnation and bondage are two deeper spiritual problems which often burden unequally-yoked wives.

If we came to Christ late in life, or wandered away from early faith, we are likely to have a lot of sin experience packed inside the baggage we brought to our marriage.

Rest assured that when you received, or returned to Christ as your Savior, all your sins were forgiven — nailed to the cross, erased from God's records. In Him, there is no longer any condemnation.

The world in which we live, however, teems with unperfected people who "remember you when." Whether or not they ever actually say so, we feel the potential is there for them to say, "Aha! I know what she's really like."

In fact, our husbands are likely the ones most skeptical about genuine change in our lives.

That sinful past is also full of triggers to call us back to a wrong lifestyle.

While we are learning to trust Christ with all our hearts, we may still reach back for the old crutches — whatever we previously used to help us deal with stress, disappointment, regrets, pain.

Identify your personal triggers so that when you face a new situation, you can say to yourself: "Christ is sufficient to overcome this. I don't need — (alcohol, a tranquilizer, a chocolate bar, a half-hour pity party)."

Then there are the bondages of besetting sins, the ones that you repeat again and again — compulsive behaviors, negative thoughts, bad mental habits like rationalization and blaming others for your faults.

Be intentional to build new habits of righteousness. Paul describes it as "putting off the old man and putting on the new man" (see Colossians 3:5-15). Make it a daily practice, just as when you put on fresh clothing.

Police your thoughts and, as II Corinthians 10:5 describes, "take them captive to the obedience of Christ" before they evolve into unrighteous words or deeds.

If we were believers who married outside the faith, we have that big, glaring sin of disobedience to deal with — and our self-condemnation will have a lot of helpers in friends and family who can now say: "I told you so!"

Think of this potential as a little gift — a good incentive to avoid complaining about him, which is one of the habits we want to change, isn't it?

I John 4:17-18 says, "Herein is our love made perfect, that we may have boldness in the day of judgment: because as he is, so are we in this world. There is no fear in love; but perfect love casteth out fear: because fear hath torment. He that feareth is not made perfect in love."

If you are continually plagued by a sense of guilt, contamination, disapproval by God or man, know that *this is not from God.* These feelings do not glorify or please Him. Let His perfect love cast out the fears that torment you, so that can be like a daughter of Sarah in I Peter 3:6 — "not afraid with any amazement."

Internal torments hinder our mission of representing the God of grace to our husbands.

So give daily attention to building your faith in what Christ has done for you until His forgiveness is as real to you as it is in God's record book. Meditate often on the sufficiency of Christ's atoning death — "knowing Christ, and Him crucified." Meet every sinful memory with the declaration: "Forgiven at the cross!"

The Lord Jesus Christ not only wants you to live in the peace of full forgiveness, but intends that in you *His joy may be full.*

Let His Light shine forth brightly from you.

AUXILIARY POWERS: STRENGTH OF CHARACTER

Besides the overall change in lives transformed by Christ, specific "powers" become more and more evident as we walk in the teachings of scripture.

Paul told his young protege Timothy, "Be strong in the *grace* that is in Christ Jesus" (II Timothy 2:1).

The New Bible Dictionary (InterVarsity Press USA, Downers Grove, Illinois 60525, 1962) says that grace "includes the idea of the *divine power* which equips a man to live a moral life" (emphasis added).

Grace is displayed in marriage by *graciousness* — courtesy, forbearing his faults, honoring him, holding him in "our good graces."

Paul talked in Philippians 4:11-13 of the power he developed through varied life experiences: "...I have learned, in whatsoever state I am, therewith *to be content.* I know both how to be abased, and I know how to abound: every where and in all things I am instructed both to be full and to be hungry, both to abound and to suffer need. *I can do all things through Christ which strengtheneth me.*"

Hand in hand with contentment is the "attitude of gratitude" — giving thanks in all circumstances: an expression of faith that our benevolent Father rules over all we face. In marriage, contentment and gratitude push complaining and whining out the door.

I Peter 3:16 speaks of the power of a *good conscience* to turn shame upon those who speak evil of you. Get rid of self-condemnation! And keep your dealings with God — confession and receiving His cleansing — up to date.

II Timothy 1:7 states, "For God hath not given us the spirit of fear; but of *power*, and of *love*, and of a *sound mind*" (emphasis added).

In Christ, we have enough power to light up our whole neighborhood!

SERVANTHOOD: THE 'SHOW' IN 'SHOW, DON'T TELL'

Doing is more meaningful to men than *saying*.

Embracing servanthood is another way to make Christ visible to our husbands — and to others.

Philippians 2:3-8 prescribes this pattern for us: "Let nothing be done through strife or vainglory; but in lowliness of mind let each esteem other better than themselves.

"Look not every man on his own things, but every man also on the things of others.

"Let this mind be in you, which was also in Christ Jesus:

"Who, being in the form of God, thought it not robbery to be equal with God:

"But made himself of no reputation, and took upon him the *form of a servant*, and was made in the likeness of men:

"And being found in fashion as a man, he humbled himself, and became obedient unto death, even the death of the cross."

Jesus Himself taught His disciples in Matthew 20:25-27 "...'Ye know that the princes of the Gentiles exercise dominion over them, and they that are great exercise authority upon them.

"'But it shall not be so among you: but whosoever will be great among you, let him be your minister;

"'And whosoever will be chief among you, let him be your servant:

"'Even as the Son of man came not to be ministered unto, but to minister, and to give his life a ransom for many.'"

We are called to *lay down our lives in service*.

James 2:18 makes a compelling argument for demonstrating faith rather than merely *talking* about it: "Yea, a man may say, Thou hast faith and I have works: shew me thy faith without thy works, and I will shew thee my faith *by* my works" (emphasis added).

Servanthood is a noble occupation. Not only are we following our Lord's example, biblical synonyms for "servant" are *deacon* and *minister.*

So — what sort of works are we talking about?

Simple things, as in Acts 9:36, 39: "...Dorcas: this woman was full of good works and almsdeeds which she did...all the widows stood by him weeping, and shewing the coats and garments which Dorcas made..."

Or, the first seven deacons who were chosen to serve tables (see Acts 6:1-6).

Or, the household administration and business enterprises of the Virtuous Woman of Proverbs 31:10-31, of whom it was said, "...let her own works praise her in the gates."

Just as a gardener knows that preparing the soil is essential to the success of his crop, a virtuous wife recognizes the need for a prepared environment for optimum human growth. Welcome, comfort, order, cleanliness, beauty, and individual privacies are essential nutrients for a happy family.

Hard work is a powerful testimony in a culture devoted to "entitlements," and your home is the place your husband will observe that work, in spite of the old joke that says "housework is what nobody notices unless you don't do it."

Housework gets a bad rap because of its sameness. But every job has its share of routine, of tediousness, of unglamourousness. Little, repetitive jobs form a great milieu to develop the spiritual fruit of *faithfulness.*

And ultimately, the patient plodder who does what is required because it is important that it be done is the woman children write poems about, the woman whose husbands refer to as "their better half," and the woman who leaves this life cushioned by warm relationships and — well, a clear conscience.

As James 2:18 says, demonstrate your faith with works. Do everything — dishes, laundry, childcare, cooking, bookkeeping, errands, yardwork, lovemaking — heartily, as unto the Lord.

And remember that skimpy preparation we discussed: "Pray, let your light shine, and leave him in God's hands"?

Don't miss this important teaching from the Lord Jesus Christ (Matthew 5:16): "Let your light so shine before men, that they may see *your good works,* and glorify your Father which is in heaven."

Servanthood portrays the One who came, not to be served, but to serve.

ℱ

BUD'S STORY: THANKSGIVING REUNION

Thanksgiving was just around the corner when Bud went into the hospital. He developed several complications from the surgery, but his doctor gave Bud a furlough to go home for the holiday. A family reunion was in the works to celebrate Bud and Lottie's 50th wedding anniversary.

Bud still suffered the mysterious pain in his legs, but he held court in his bedroom. His kids went in two by two to talk with him. When they leaned down to kiss him, he cupped their faces in both hands — a never-before-experienced caress.

His appetite had begun to falter, but his older son lifted him into Lottie's swivel desk chair and rolled him into the dining room.

Harriet, the Family Churchwoman, usually asked the Lord's blessing on Thanksgiving dinner.

She had already taken her place at the intersection of kitchen, dining room and living room when Bud spoke up.

"I'll say grace," he said.

The 24 people gathered around the four tables it took to seat them were startled into silence.

Bud bowed his head and said, "Lord, make us thankful for these and all our many blessings. Amen."

The silence continued after the Amen. Bud's prayer wasn't the standard blessing his children had recited over the years ("God is great, God is good, and we thank Him for this food"), but one he had apparently learned at his mother's table.

In a merry mood, Bud managed to eat a full plate of dressing and gravy.

The only prayer the family had ever heard Bud pray was answered immediately — they *were* thankful for their many blessings.

EXERCISE 1
LET PATIENCE HAVE HER PERFECT WORK - PART 2

The Amplified New Testament (Family Library, New York NY by arrangement with Zondervan Publishing House, May 1973) renders James 1:3-4 thus: "Be assured and understand that the trial and proving of your faith bring out endurance and steadfastness and patience. But let endurance and steadfastness and patience have full play and do a thorough work, so that you may be (people) perfectly and fully developed (with no defects), lacking in nothing."

This brings out two aspects of patience

- ACTIVE, which is persistence or steadfastness

and

- PASSIVE, which is endurance

1. Which seems harder for you — to steadfastly pursue, through prayer or work, an elusive outcome? (What things, besides your husband's salvation, fit into this category?)

-
-
-
-

2. OR is it harder for you to endure repeatedly broken promises, your mate's bad habits, children who play you against your husband, irritating comments from churchgoers who speculate about your divided marriage? List your other "patience trials":

-
-
-
-

Take heart! You will be perfected through both kinds of trials if you let patience have her work —don't waste the experience!

EXERCISE 2
PRESENTING A VISUAL WITNESS

Read I Peter 3:1-6 with I Corinthians 2:1-5.

1. How does the I Peter passage speak of presenting a visual witness?

2. How did Paul describe his preaching method in the I Corinthians passage?

3. What are practical ways we can present a visual witness in our homes?

- new habits
- standing for righteousness
- silence when wronged
-
-
-

4. Consider the following scriptures for other ideas:

- I Corinthians 13:4-7, 11
- II Corinthians 3:2-3, 7-9, 18
- Galatians 5:16-26
- James 2:18

EXERCISE 3
PORTRAIT OF A 'WINNING WIFE'

Chaste: pure in thought and heart, being prepared for Christ, her eternal Bridegroom. See: II Corinthians 11:2, I Thessalonians 4:7, II Timothy 2: 20-22, Titus 2:5, James 3:17, I John 3:3

Coupled with fear (of displeasing): trustworthy, a faithful worker, intent on blessing her husband and family. See: Proverbs 18:22, Proverbs 19:14, Proverbs 31:11-12 and 30-31

Gentle spirit: free of anger, vengefulness, backbiting

Quiet spirit: at rest in the Lord, at peace in her household, not distracted by "so many things," but focussed on what is needful

Unafraid: trusting in the Lord, confident in her husband

Submissive: cooperative, honoring husband's God-appointed leadership

Respectful: her fundamental attitude

A good helpmeet: reliable, protects her husband's reputation with people outside the home and his authority inside the home

Righteous: the exception to obeying a husband: "do not participate in sin." See: I Timothy 5:22

Beautifying the "hidden man of the heart": internalizing the winning ways so that what the husband sees in our outward behavior, the Lord sees in our hearts. See: II Corinthians 5:12 and Colossians 3:22

Fearing the Lord: recognizing her accountability to God. See: Proverbs 31:30 and Colossians 3:23-24

EXERCISE 4
DISCOVERY AND PRAYER PROJECT: AM I A GOOD HELPMEET?

1. Am I discontent with my role as my husband's helper? Why?
___ God should have made allowances for American culture and equal opportunity.
___ My husband doesn't want my help.
___ I'm too busy with my own life to stretch any further.
___ My abilities and insights are superior to my husband's in most areas.
___ I am the one who hears from God. I should be in charge.

2. Do I "overdo" my helpfulness by anticipating his decisions and getting ahead of him?
___ Do I nag or "mother" him?
___ Do I choose the ways I am willing to help, or do I discern where he is struggling and complement his weaknesses?
___ Do I give him freedom to fail?
___ Do I keep quiet if he fails because he didn't follow my counsel?

3. Do I put on a good act while plotting ways to get around his stated or known desires?

4. Do I truly see my husband as God's instrument to make me like Christ?

5. Can I make the connection that submitting to my husband is actually equivalent to submitting to the Lord?

6. Even so, I am morally responsible to God. Are there areas in my marriage where I need to take a stand contrary to my husband's leading? (See Acts 5:29 and Colossians 3:18).

Pray for God's grace in dealing with these issues.

EXERCISE 5
CLEAN YOUR HANDS!

Look up the following scriptures, and consider how they apply to the work of household ministry:

1. II Samuel 22:21-25

2. Job 17:9

3. Psalm 18:20-24

4. Psalm 24:3-4

5. Proverbs 12:24

6. Proverbs 14:1

7. Proverbs 30:32

Now — read Colossians 3:1, and then think about what it means to be your husband's "right hand."

EXERCISE 6
ANGER: TAME IT, TRANSFORM IT

Read Genesis 4:5-7 and Ephesians 4:26-27. Anger is Satan's doorway to provoke us to sin. Learn from your anger. Consciously or subconsciously, your husband knows how to take you out of control by pushing the right "hot buttons." You need to know how to disarm those buttons, and not "give place to the devil."

Think about your last experience of anger. Exactly what happened, exactly what fears or other feelings were aroused?

Is there an ongoing problem on the other party's side? Anything that needs to be confronted and resolved? If so, how can you "speak the truth in love?"

On the other hand, did you provoke the angry exchange in some way? Do you have a pattern of behavior — a "blind spot" — that annoys or angers your mate? Examine your own heart. If you're not sure, "*ask* for the truth in love" as a child of God: a peacemaker (see Matthew 5:9).

What mitigating factors on your side make you easily angered: hormonal cycles, fatigue, pain? Can you do a quick calculation to divide the blame and lessen your angry response?

What mitigating factors are at play in your spouse? Fatigue, pain, worry, displaced anger against another person? Cut him a little slack, and show him your grace.

Now — take that big bundle of energy and use it for something productive.

Remember that the Prince of Peace resides within you — give Him lots of elbow room, and get a good night's sleep.

CHAPTER 8

Communication

The Neglected Art

BUD'S STORY: A NEW KIND OF RELATIONSHIP

Bud's leg pain persisted, so his doctor scheduled a repeat surgery. It provided very little relief, but the doctor said he couldn't do any more for him at the hospital. He would need physical therapy at home.

Lottie and two of her children drove to the hospital to pick him up. During the drive home, he suffered a stroke.

Back to the hospital they went.

The family gathered, and spent weeks at bedside vigil. Bud couldn't speak or swallow, or move his right limbs, although he often surprised the family with his independence and resourcefulness at making his needs known. His children took turns shaving him, applying lotion to his hands and his handsome, bald head, cleaned his teeth with swabs, applied glycerin to moisten his mouth and nostrils.

They held his left hand so he could squeeze theirs to communicate.

A year earlier, their ministrations would have humiliated Bud, but now he submitted gratefully. It answered, at last, their need to be close to him.

⁂

TIMING IS EVERYTHING

Ecclesiastes 3:1, 7 says: "To every thing there is a season, and a time to every purpose under the heaven...a time to keep silence, and a time to speak."

A wise woman — the home builder — learns when to keep silence, and when to speak.

SILENCE IS GOLDEN

I Peter 3:1-6 reminds us that missionary wives are supposed to give their most powerful witness with their behavior rather than with their words. Our challenge is to exhibit the right kind of *doing* and let our husbands infer the spiritual message.

Jesus Himself remarked that "a prophet is not without honour, save in his own country, and in his own house" (Matthew 13:57).

We have not always been honorable in our homes. We have used our tongues for both blessing and cursing.

Because we are the less-powerful, or weaker, sex, our tendency is to use words as weapons. We have been known to critique, belittle, manipulate, deceive, disrespect to get our own way, or to make an emphatic point.

It takes a lot of credibility-building for us to persuade a husband to trust that our tongue is now an instrument of grace, love and truth.

Then, preaching can come back and bite us. When you give out "the word," you will put yourself on the defensive. Our husbands will note: "You *said* (this or that), and yet you are *doing* (something *other* than this or that)." Or, they'll ask that famous question that could be the slogan of Unbelieving Husbands United:

"Is that how a Christian acts?"

Preaching puts a wife into the role of spiritual leader. And it would be an awful sacrifice to give up that position once her husband became a Christian! It would be like getting a demotion for accomplishing a good work.

Keep in mind: *argument* is not as compelling as *evidence*.

A 'QUIET SPIRIT' SPEAKS VOLUMES

A woman with a quiet spirit doesn't complain. Philippians 2:14-15 says, "Do all things without murmurings and disputings:

"That ye may be blameless and harmless, the sons of God, without rebuke, in the midst of a crooked and perverse nation, among whom *ye shine as lights in the world*" (emphasis added).

A woman with a quiet spirit isn't argumentative — as opposed to the example in Proverbs 27:15: "A continual dropping in a very rainy day and a contentious woman are alike."

She doesn't nag — a practice which raises resentment and stubbornness in her husband.

I Peter 3:4 describes a quiet spirit as "an ornament." It is of great price in the sight of God because it evidences a woman's faith in Him. He is the One on whom she can rely in every circumstance. He is her confidence, her strength, her dignity.

She isn't a nonstop chatterer, afraid to let a moment of silence intrude into a conversation. She is the woman to whom other people say, "You're so restful to be around."

PARTICULAR 'COMMUNICATIONS' TO AVOID:

Our husbands are likely to be offended rather than impressed with the accoutrements we women love: Christian bumper stickers, wall plaques and door mats with inspirational sayings, the WWJD ("What would Jesus do?") bracelet, other esoteric jewelry, scripture-verse adorned ball point pens and coffee mugs — even "Christian" breath mints.

Instead, like Paul, we should glory in the cross.

That doesn't mean that you only display knickknacks that feature a cross — but that you live a life centered on the cross of Christ: overridingly conscious of Whose you are — a sinner purchased by the Lord Jesus Christ with His own precious blood — and what you are about: appointed to infect others with eternal life by pointing them to Christ in *the most effective way.*

An analogy to glorying in the cross would be the soldier who "fights for his flag" — his whole sense of mission is focussed on the people and the values that flag represents.

Our mission is to "live for the cross" — focussed on the Person and the values His sacrifice represents.

DON'T FLAUNT YOUR 'CHRISTIANESE'

Although Americans are typically language-poor among other developed nations in our world, we have our own form of multi-lingualism.

We speak "girl talk" or "guy talk."

We have vocational lingo, and vocabularies which betray our ethnic heritage or regional origins.

We have "body language" — rolling our eyes, smirking, curling our lips, crossing our arms tightly across the chest — which almost anyone can translate,

And most churchgoers speak "Christianese," which may be harder to figure out.

Christianese includes strange expressions like "I covet your prayers," "You need to get in the Word," "I'm looking for the Rapture," "I'm starving for fellowship," "We did battle in the heavenlies."

It's delicious to be among those who speak the same language we do — but it's uncomfortable to be stuck in a group where you are the ignorant outsider.

One reason to use verbal evangelism sparingly with our husbands is that things that are special to us about our faithlife and churchlife — and the terms we use to describe them — are meaningless to them.

Keep in mind when you do engage in a spiritual discussion with your husband that "Christianese" is usually an irritant to a nonChristian.

VIVE LA DIFFERENCE!

In the musical "My Fair Lady," Professor Henry Higgins sings, "Why Can't A Woman Be More Like A Man?"

The feminist movement over the past two generations has aimed to answer that plea — and also to "make a man be more like a woman."

The coarsening of womanhood and the feminization of our men has introduced a new level of confusion into human relations, in our churches as well as in secular society. Men are tentative about taking authority — women are not at all timid about usurping it.

But our attempts to talk to our husbands about our faith may fizzle simply because men and women generally don't see things the same way. There are still innate gender differences that missionary wives need to hold in mind.

In general:

Men's primary information receptors are their eyes; women receive through their ears, and to a degree through their intuition. Women can "believe a report" or sense information that is not visibly apparent. Men tend to be like the disciple Thomas: "Unless I see..."

Men are "big picture" oriented, while most women are detail-oriented.

Men are task-oriented, women are people-oriented.

Men may resort to force — verbal or physical — to get their way; women use persuasion and influence (or deceit and manipulation) to get theirs.

Men demonstrate their love through the things they do; women like to verbalize their love. Our expectations similarly differ: men would like to *see* our works; we long to *hear* their declarations of devotion.

Men and women don't read the same kinds of books. Books that I "couldn't put down" are often ones my Christian brothers "couldn't get into."

Men are more likely to be interested in a message which presents Christ as a Hero rather than a Buddy, One who challenges them rather than soothes them.

For example, our comfort in "the everlasting arms" (Deuteronomy 33:27) is not what men are usually in the market for — just as "by thee I have run through a troop; by my God have I leaped over a wall" (2 Samuel 22:30) is not high on *a woman's* list of desires.

Male and female He created us — so "get wisdom and understanding" rather than getting mad because your husband can't see things the way you see them.

WHEN IT'S OKAY TO SPEAK OUT

People who know I am a practicing Christian will sometimes ask me to say a prayer before a shared meal, even when my husband is in the group.

I am always honored to be asked, and my husband doesn't object. I keep it short and sweet. (In fact, I think the reason my husband doesn't object when I pray is because he's had to endure other pray-ers who take the opportunity to catch up on their private prayer lives or to preach at everyone else at the table.)

Unless you have been specifically asked not to, I think it is within your role as parent to teach your children to return thanks before meals — short and sweet! — and to end the day with a bedtime prayer when you tuck them in. This is a good time to guide them to confess sin, express thanksgiving, and to ask God's blessing on family and friends.

My husband has overheard me praying on the telephone when someone calls with a problem; he has "caught me" at prayer by coming home unexpectedly when I'm on my knees. That's not a huge problem, either.

But I believe we should confine our *emotional* prayer times to a place of privacy (the "prayer closet" Jesus recommended) or to church, rather than making a display that will cause unbelieving family members discomfort.

Your husband will know you are a praying woman without having to see you on the job.

AND PRAYER IS THE PROPER PLACE TO BEGIN YOUR 'SPEAKING'

Years ago, I heard a little verse which has stayed with me:

I cannot speak to you of God,
Since worldly-wise you grew,
And so, with teardrops in my eyes,
I speak to God of you.

Pray is our Godward work as household missionaries.

James 1:5 prescribes: "If any of you lack wisdom, let him ask of God..."

This is the daily supply we need at our mission field. Seek God's wisdom continually. His ways are always better — more effective — than our ways.

We and God are in this missionary business together, and so we pray to unite our purposes with His. We seek our husbands' salvation

- to glorify Jesus
- to connect Him with one of the trophies He died for
- to reconcile a lost sheep with his Shepherd.

Jesus instructed us to pray: "*Thy kingdom come, Thy will be done, on earth as it is in heaven.*"

Salvation is God's will.

We should ever be on the alert for other scriptures to pray — you'll find a get-started list in an exercise at the back of this chapter.

In earlier exercises, you have already discovered many specific petitions to pray — for God's help to remove the hindrances we bring to the situation, and for His intervention in removing hindrances we can't affect, like our husbands' history of bad church experiences, or exposure to hypocritical Christians, or the topics they get hung up on as barriers to belief: creation versus evolution, for example.

James again has this great encouragement (James 5:16) "...The effectual fervent prayer of a righteous man availeth much."

BUILD COMMUNICATION IN OTHER AREAS

Spiritual division in a marriage can create the sense that the couple has nothing to talk about.

That Jesus is called "The Word" indicates to me that love and communication are intimately joined. It's critical that we maintain friendship with our husbands — meeting conversationally around shared interests and problems.

Sometimes a husband's hindrance is jealousy of God. He needs to know he is valuable to his wife.

I used to put on a smug, "God-will-provide-for-me-whether-you-do-or-not" attitude, thinking I was proclaiming my faith. But it actually indicated to my husband that he was a fifth wheel in my life.

God provides through people. And His number one choice as a wife's provider is her husband — not only to provide material needs, but tenderness, comradeship, protection, security, and appreciation as well.

So, if you're in short supply of any of these things, make your requests known to your husband, as you would make them known to God: not accusingly, whiningly, or demandingly, but in a humble, honest, grateful and trusting expression of need.

There is no end of topics we can discuss with our mates:

- our shared social lives: planning ways to spend time with friends, supporting them in times of need
- our finances: goals, adjustments we need to make
- vocations — is everybody happy with the demands of our employment? If not, what can be changed?
- extended family: building relationships with in-laws, meeting needs, defining boundaries
- our children: discipline and other problems, activity planning, character goals, educational goals and the budgeting required, how to teach life skills, emergency preparedness, standards for companions and entertainments
- household management, division of labor
- leisure activities

Keep a lively flow of conversation between you. Stay "on the same page" with your husband in the many matters that pertain to both of you.

LISTENING: THE NEGLECTED ELEMENT IN CONVERSATION

Someone (probably a man) has pointed out that God gave us two ears and only one mouth: therefore we should do twice as much listening as speaking.

I'm pretty sure your husband will be more agreeable to conversing with you frequently if you let him get a word in edgewise now and then.

We who are seekers after wisdom face a particular danger in thinking we know more than our pagan spouses. Even without our gift of intuition, they will pick up the sense that we are not all that interested in their input.

Wrong signal to send!

Remember all the differences inherent in "male and female created He them"? Most husbands are very good problem solvers when they are allowed to brainstorm — and keep in mind that "split-screen" image of the One who may be speaking through your mate.

Another advantage to keep in mind is Jesus' comment, "...out of the abundance of the heart the mouth speaketh" (Matthew 12:34). Welcome every opportunity to let your man reveal "his heart." Listen to him respectfully and attentively.

If your communication with your husband is comfortable, your heart will also speak, in a natural, unthreatening, "unpreachy" way.

WHAT ABOUT INDIRECT 'PREACHING?'

If you maintain good relationships with your husband's unbelieving friends, it's possible that one of them may begin to show spiritual interest.

If he asks you questions in front of your husband, enter a silent undercurrent of prayer and answer freely. Your husband may choose to walk away, but if not, speak on anyway!

You have a good opportunity to lay out the core elements of the gospel to his friend, and indirectly, to your husband.

Some cautions apply, however. Don't be baited into nasty arguments about side issues — you are not likely to change his mind until God changes his heart. Keep turning the conversation to the gospel:

- God loves people, whom He created for relationship with Himself
- Sin is the problem that spoils the plan
- Jesus is the remedy.

On the other hand, beware of becoming a spiritual mother to your husband's friend. It is too intimate a connection. Instead, give him books or tapes to help with his questions. If he is genuinely interested, introduce him to a Christian brother or to your pastor.

Sometimes spiritual interest is a come-on to gain a sympathetic ear. Don't become his counselor by trying to meet his emotional needs. That will create a bigger divide between you and your husband, and between the friend and your husband — not to mention causing problems with the friend's wife, if he has one.

Get wisdom — it is the principal thing in all of life.

WHAT ABOUT YOUR CHILDREN'S QUESTIONS?

When you and your husband discuss your children, put forward a case for taking them to Sunday school or midweek church youth programs. While acknowledging the religious content they will receive, point out the virtue of their developing wholesome friendships and moral values.

Don't despair if he balks at your proposal. He may have had bad church experiences in his youth. He may have been turned off by less-than-ethical practices he has seen by businessmen whom he knows to be churchgoers.

Of course, there are sometimes wolves among the sheep. Pray constantly for your children and, if your husband has reservations about any of the activities, let him rule.

If he has no legitimate reasons to resist, wait patiently. Proverbs 21:1 says, "The king's heart is in the hand of the Lord, as the rivers of water: he turneth it whithersoever he will."

Rather than entering into battle to change his mind, let God change his heart.

At home, try to answer your children's questions in front of your husband, rather than holding "secret meetings" with them. Answer their questions honestly, again using that undercurrent of prayer for wisdom.

Never disparage your husband to your children over his lack of belief.

PREPARING TO ANSWER YOUR HUSBAND'S QUESTIONS

There may come a time when your husband will begin to show interest in learning a little more about your faith. I Peter 3:15 tells us, "...be ready always to give an answer to every man that asketh you a reason of the hope that is in you with meekness and fear."

God's Holy Spirit will teach you, and will bring the teachings to mind, provided you have exposed yourself to them through study, study, study of God's Word. Colossians 3:16 says, "Let the word of Christ *dwell* in you richly in all wisdom...."

Have a reasoned faith. Clarify your own testimony. Just exactly why are you a believer?

When your husband asks questions, give him a thoughtful answer.

And don't get into debates about creation, Noah's ark, where Cain's wife came from. Just say, regarding contentious questions, "I accept God's entire word, but this issue is not the heart of the gospel."

When you speak to him:

- speak humbly, not with an "I-know-it-all" attitude
- speak quietly, unemotionally — calm assurance carries conviction
- speak lovingly — you are not trying to win an argument, but a soul.

ODD WAYS HE MAY COMMUNICATE WITH YOU

Evidence of your husband's spiritual interest may not be all that pleasant. The heavy hand of conviction may manifest itself in bad temper, belittling remarks, and a fierce interest in looking for "some other way" of relating to God than through Christianity — delving into psychology, philosophy, and bizarre, joyless religions.

This is the time to let patience have her perfecting work — in both of you. Keep praying for God to open your husband's spiritual eyes to recognize Jesus, the Bread of Life, as the answer to his spiritual hunger.

HOW DO YOU KNOW, O WIFE, WHETHER YOU WILL WIN YOUR HUSBAND?

Bud had another stroke. The family gathered at his bedside in the intensive care unit, a few people at a time, where Bud showed no cognizance of their presence.

Bud lived six more weeks, incommunicado, still registering pain in the one leg that wasn't paralyzed.

He was moved to a private room, where visitors were not so restricted. The family made a rotating schedule to ensure that he had company and an advocate as often as possible.

Three of his kids were bold enough to pray aloud for him, and one read scripture to him every time she was on duty, declaring what Christ had done for his sake.

He was never able to respond — so far as the family could tell.

Bud died the day Harriet finalized the purchase of a house in her hometown. She and her husband planned to retire in a couple of years, and wanted to live close to Lottie.

EXERCISE 1
LOOK ON THE FIELD:
WHERE DOES COMMUNICATION BREAK DOWN?

- What annoys your husband?

- What makes him indignant?

- Angry?

- Sarcastic?

- How does he close down communication? (Saying that he doesn't want to talk about something? giving you the silent treatment? leaving the house?)

- What things does he fear?

- What does he worry about?

- What does he not worry about, that you think he should?

- What does he admire, respect, worship?

- What are the desires of his heart?

- What energizes him?

- What subjects turn him on conversationally?

Make it your daily prayer and your daily practice to seek God's help in enhancing good conversation in your marriage. Pray that God will help you become an enthusiastic and creative worker with Him in building your marriage.

EXERCISE 2
CLARIFY YOUR TESTIMONY

What do you believe — and why? I Peter 3:15 says, "But sanctify the Lord God in your hearts: and *be ready always to give an answer* to every man that asketh you a reason of the hope that is in you with meekness and fear."

Analyze your own beliefs, and how you arrived at them.

For example:

- God made Himself real to me by ______________________________.
- I felt the longevity of the Christian faith gave it credence, so I investigated its claims by (reading scripture or a recommended book, attending a revival...)
- I was attracted by the life of a godly friend or family member
- I was looking for purpose and meaning in my life
- I needed to deal with a sorrowful event or a sinful past

Then: what was the pivotal experience that brought you to receive Christ as your Savior?

And now:

How has your life changed since you became rightly related to the God who loves you?

- victory over a bad habit
- repaired relationships
- answered prayers
-
-
-

Colossians 4:6 says, "Let your speech be alway with grace, seasoned with salt, that ye may know how ye ought to answer every man." Which parts of your testimony do you think would be "how you ought to answer" your husband?

EXERCISE 3
WHAT IS 'THE GOSPEL?"

Gospel means "good news!"

God is love. He created us to share a life of love with Himself and with each other.

BUT, God is holy and sinless, and we are not. He has no fellowship with darkness.

The problem is our sin, which includes:

- evil thoughts and deeds
- rebellion: the attitude that says, "Nobody's going to tell me what to do!"
- unbelief: atheism, cynicism, exaltation of *proof* and *reason.* Faith encompasses unseen things, and requires spiritual discernment.

Faith is a MISSING PIECE until a man is born again of the Spirit (see John 3:3).

Only God could solve the problem of our separation from Him. He did it by incarnation, identifying with the human race by taking on human flesh as Jesus, who was fully man, yet also fully God.

He took all of the sins of the world — including every one of ours — upon Himself at the time of His execution, where God's penalty against sin was satisfied. God raised Him from the dead and His followers are raised into "newness of life" in the present age as well as into eternal life.

We partake of this good news by simply believing what God has done to redeem us. The evidence that we are "born again" grows as we bow to His will for our lives and allow Him to change our thoughts and behaviors.

EXERCISE 4
'ALL YOU CAN DO IS PRAY...'
PROMISES AND PATTERNS TO PRAY FOR YOUR FAMILY

Matthew 9:29 - "...According to your faith be it unto you."

Matthew 9:37-38- "Then saith he unto his disciples, 'The harvest truly is plenteous, but the labourers are few;

"'Pray ye therefore the Lord of the harvest, that he will send forth labourers into his harvest."

Mark 11:24 - "Therefore I say unto you, What things soever ye desire, when ye pray, believe that ye receive them, and ye shall have them."

Luke 19:10 - "For the Son of Man is come to seek and save that which was lost."

John 15:7 - "If ye abide in me, and my words abide in you, ye shall ask what ye will, and it shall be done unto you."

Ephesians 1:17-18 - "That the God of our Lord Jesus Christ, the Father of glory, may give unto (our family members) the spirit of wisdom and revelation in the knowledge of him:

"The eyes of (their) undertanding being enlightened; that (they) may know what is the hope of his calling, and what the riches of the glory of his inheritance in the saints."

I Timothy 1:15 - "This is a faithful saying, and worthy of all acceptation, that Christ Jesus came into the world to save sinners...."

Hebrews 8:12 - "For I will be merciful to their unrighteousness, and their sins and their iniquities will I remember no more."

II Peter 3:9 "The Lord is not slack concerning his promise, as some men count slackness; but is longsuffering to us-ward, not willing that any should perish, but that all should come to repentance."

EXERCISE 5
WHAT ARE WE SUPPOSED TO SHOW HIM?

1. Show him that he is a person of great worth.

2. Show him the benefits you receive through your walk with the Lord:
- contentment regardless of circumstances
- the mood-elevating "joy of the Lord"
- the deep settled peace of a quiet spirit
- an attitude of gratitude
- the freedom of a clear conscience
- your growth in holiness and purity as the Lord changes your preferences
- your freedom from fear (what, me worry?)
- your readiness to meet needs through serving others — especially him!
- steady grace: slow to take offense and quick to forgive
- unfaltering respect for him

Evidence is more compelling than argument!

EXERCISE 6
STRATEGIC POWER: TONGUE CONTROL

Proverbs 18:21 says, "Death and life are in the power of the tongue...."

Copy the following verses from your favorite bible, and consider how they apply in your marriage:

Psalm 15:1-3 -

Proverbs 6:16-19 -

Proverbs 15:1-2 -

Proverbs 28:23 -

Proverbs 31:26 -

Romans 12:1 -

Ephesians 4:29 -

Ephesians 5:19-20 -

I Peter 3:10 -

What are some sins of the tongue?

How can the tongue be an instrument of blessing

- to God?
- to your family?

Pray for God to help you tame this "unruly member" and dedicate it to the power of life.

CHAPTER 9

Blessed to Bless

The Neglected Distribution

LOTTIE AND HARRIET, TOGETHER AGAIN

By the time Harriet and her husband moved home to New Mexico, Lottie had come to terms with widowhood. She lived alone in her big house filled with its memories.

She still had nothing to do with church. "I don't have any church clothes — my feet are too old for dress shoes — I wouldn't even know how to act in church, after all these years," she'd say.

Harriet and her sister-in-law enrolled in Bible Study Fellowship, and they talked Lottie into joining them.

Lottie loved it, spending hours completing her homework, getting re-acquainted with her bible. She was captivated by the young teaching leader who delivered the weekly lecture. She became friends with many of the women in her discussion group.

But her health began to wane after the first year.

She had regained a spiritual hunger, however. She found a television preacher whose teachings she liked.

WE ARE BLESSED TO BLESS OTHERS

We are *separated to a work.* Our lives are focussed on serving one man as God's ambassador. We are "Saint Wife" at our home address.

We are not, however, *isolated* from the universal church of the Lord Jesus Christ, or from the larger world we inhabit.

Our training, our growth in wisdom and virtue, our close fellowship with our indwelling Savior, equips us to serve God and to serve people in untold ways.

God said in Genesis 18:17-19, "...Shall I hide from Abraham that thing which I do;

"Seeing that Abraham shall surely become a great and mighty nation, and all the nations of the earth shall be blessed in him?

"For I know him, that he will command his children and his household after him, and they shall keep the way of the Lord, to do justice and judgment: that the Lord may bring upon Abraham that which he hath spoken of him."

All nations are blessed from a faith that started in one household — not only the nations of Abraham's lifetime, but you and I are blessed as well.

Galatians 3:7 says, "Know ye therefore that they which are of faith, the same are the children of Abraham."

We are blessed by God to pass His blessings on, and in God's abundant economy, one believer can affect innumerable others.

Unless — like the timid steward in Jesus' Parable of the Talents (Matthew 25:14-30) — you bury what God has entrusted to you rather than investing it for His profit.

What will God do with your faith, missionary wife? Who will be blessed because God has blessed you?

JESUS IS BLESSED BY OUR LIVES

Our blessings pour down through Jesus, the True Vine to whom we are joined in a living relationship.

We *develop friendship with Him* through obedience: "Ye are my friends, if ye do whatsoever I command you" (John 15:14).

We *share His yoke* as we learn His teachings: "Take my yoke upon you, and learn of me; for I am meek and lowly in heart: and ye shall find rest unto your souls" (Matthew 11:29).

We *please Him* with that quiet spirit that evidences our faith.

We are His beloved, the ones He died for, the ones He is preparing a place for, the ones He will come again for, and take us to that prepared place, where we will be with Him forever.

We are joined to Him in everlasting love!

WE BLESS OUR HUSBANDS

For all his seeming lack of sensitivity, a man's sense of self-worth depends on the assurance that he is loved — that he is worthy of love.

A wife can demoralize him with complaints, arguments, always needing to have the last word, comparing him unfavorably with other men (especially with such paragons as her pastor), and her discontent. Proverbs 12:25 says, "Heaviness in the heart of man maketh it stoop: but a good word maketh it glad."

One man, who had struggled for years before he finally closed the business he had created, said his wife's reaction was a repetition of the many times she had said: "I told you so!"

He said, "She made me hate myself."

It is not our job to make our husbands humble. It is our job to "hearten" them — to put heart into them, not to take it out.

And to *empower* them.

When my husband and I go to the election polls, we often vote for opposing candidates and cancel each other's vote. When we vote for the same person, however, we double the impact on that candidate's showing.

This is how it works when we yield our "power" to our husbands — we double his strength. When we oppose him, we cancel it.

A wife also blesses her husband by being his friend — preferring his company, keeping a healthy flow of communication with him, helping him be his best self.

Knowing that you are on his side — a "friend who loveth at all times," as Proverbs 17:17 says —is a tremendously beneficial salve to ease his problems and difficulties. And you will benefit with good family morale, the lessening of family tension, and the knowledge that you are a direct contributor to your husband's efficient functioning.

Friends are loyal. We represent him well to other people.

My aunt once attended an elegant tea party, where she was a virtual stranger among the guests. A haughty matron approached her and nodded a greeting. "How do you do," she said. "I'm Mrs. Webster — the banker's wife."

Auntie stood tall, nodded back, and said, "I'm happy to meet you. I'm Mrs. Johnson — the barber's wife."

She made it clear that she was the wife of a very fine barber.

Make your husband *your* hero.

We need also to represent him in heaven with our faithful, strategic, fervent, effectual prayers.

THE SLEEPING GIANT?

Could our spiritually-dormant husbands be the "sleeping giant" that can lead the church back to its role as the moral preservative of our society?

Are they the force — manly, secure, supported in love — who can counter the cultural forces that threaten the church from without and from within?

How could God bless the world through your husband — as He blesses your husband through you?

How is God blessing the world through him now? What contributions is he making through his vocation? His parenting? By being a good neighbor, a good Samaritan to a stranger in distress?

Thank God for using him as an agent of blessing in all the ways He is.

BLESSING OUR CHILDREN

Rearing a child to bear personal responsibility for his life is no mean task. It's manifestly more difficult in an age where cultural values are so peculiar. Rather than supporting the beneficial structure of authority, the paramount interest today is rights — yes, even for children. Children are often the ones governing their parents and their teachers, rather than the other way around.

With bizarre dangers on every hand, from harmful toys, the "sensory overkill" of television and movie entertainment, the patterning of violence in video games, internet porn — and internet predators — illegal drugs and overprescribed legal drugs — the role of protector is a major task for parents.

Impermanence is also a threat to a child's sense of security. We are a mobile society, so children are often required to adjust to new circumstances: moving away from a best friend, from a special hideout — perhaps from a parent, when divorce rocks his world.

And when a mom turns to Christ (or a husband turns away from him), the dynamics of the home change for everyone in it. Spiritual division can be very confusing for a couple's children.

The amount of influence a Christian wife can impose on her children's belief will vary with the degree of her husband's opposition to Christianity.

If he is merely indifferent to spiritual matters, he may not care if she teaches songs and prayers and scripture verses to their children, if she buys them their own bibles and Christian story books and videos.

If he is hostile toward God and church, however, or if he is a member of a non-Christian religion, he may resist any proselytizing of his children.

Talk to God first. Then talk to your husband, and be clear what the limits are from his point of view.

Then ask him to help find points of agreement on what values are important to transmit to them.

Bear in mind that you will probably not be one-hundred percent happy with the results of your first discussion.

But that's okay. Re-visit the issue weeks or months later. God may soften him, especially if you accept his early ruling with good grace and compliance.

Do resolve that you will not disrespect your husband to your children by badmouthing his lack of faith or different faith. Don't indicate that he is a villain when he says "no" to a church event you really wanted your children to attend.

The goals you can probably agree on from the start are to teach:

- obedience
- respect for authority
- truthfulness and honesty
- personal responsibility
- taking care of possessions
- sharing possessions, and
- contributing to the work of the home.

It's a good beginning. You can teach these values without invoking the name of Jesus — but Jesus would approve of them.

In addition, you should agree on guidelines for discipline.

MAKE LOVE THE SUBSTANCE OF YOUR RELATIONSHIP

As with your husband, the most important thing to teach your child is a sense of self-worth — a sane sense! It's just as bad to give a child the idea that the world — or even the family — revolves around him as it is to make him believe he's the Great Affliction.

Love gives him that sense of self-worth. And that is where you can quietly impart God into his life by loving him as God does.

We can always count on God's love as a *fact*. It is not withdrawn by our bad behavior, not made visible only in response to our good behavior. It is the substance of our relationship.

If we were servants, God could fire and rehire us according to our merit or performance, but we are His own children, and His love for us is unconditional.

God does have standards for us, however. They are designed specifically for our deepest happiness and growth into maturity. His expectations are clearly set forth in His Holy Word.

A mother needs to make love for each child the substance of their relationship by letting them know she's glad to see them everytime she does — when they get up in the morning, when they come home from school — even when they come home way past curfew. Then, when the next item on the agenda is scolding, it is more likely to provoke the child's regret than anger or defensiveness.

For their ultimate happiness and growth to maturity, they also need the security of limits, as God has provided for us.

A mother needs to

- set standards of behavior — the ones you and your husband have agreed upon
- express them clearly
- oversee compliance
- correct when needed, and
- praise appropriately.

Parental praise is important to everyone. Even the Lord Jesus Christ heard the words: "This is my beloved Son, in Whom I am well pleased" from His Father.

There's a real hunger for positive feedback from one's parents and, as with other hungers, if it isn't satisfied, growth is stunted.

A retired pediatric dentist recently wrote to "Dear Abby" about a 5-year-old patient he had seen for a dental emergency. The youngster had been upset when he arrived, but the dentist gave him a hug, and when he finished, he complimented the youngster for his behavior.

The dentist scheduled a follow-up appointment for the boy the following week.

When they returned, the boy's grandmother, who was raising him in the stead of a teenage mother who had abandoned him, told the dentist that the boy had jumped out of bed every morning asking, "Is this the day we go back to the dentist?"

When the dentist inquired why he was so eager to return, she said, "Because you told him he was a good boy."

Do discriminate between praise, which encourages, and flattery, which "puffs up," however.

"You're such a cute little boy!" is okay for love-talk when you're cuddling him or greeting him when you wake him up, but it won't really do him a service to exclaim, "I wouldn't let you get away with that if you weren't so cute," or "how cute!" when he says something sassy or does something outrageous to get attention.

Praise him for behavior that is consistent with the values you and your husband have established. "You've done a nice job of keeping your room neat this week!" "Your math grade has gone up — your extra studying has paid off, and I'm very proud of you!" Give him sincere evaluation of his performance and your approval.

And, just as with your husband, you can do lots of teaching "without a word" — by good example. (Did you keep your room neat this week?)

Are your children positively influenced by your choice of friends, your leisure activities, the priorities you honor? The way you maintain your relationships?

The other side of the coin, of course, is discipline for wrongdoing — and it's an important element of love. In fact, love is the whole point of discipline. You want your child to grow up to be a worthwile, happy person, and your job is to correct his course when he does things which divert him from that path. Discipline in sorrow, not in anger because you've been offended by his disobedience.

And do call trangressions by their proper names, not euphemisms. Don't say, "It isn't nice to borrow money from mother's purse." Say, "Taking money that belongs to somebody else is stealing." Help him learn to identify and confess his sin, and to make restitution when possible.

COUNSELING AGAINST THE UNEQUAL YOKE

Duh!

Discuss dating standards before children begin to date. Whether or not your child has made a commitment to Christ, the issue of spiritual agreement should be held up as a positive value.

And, I believe that when you have that "facts of life" talk with your teen is a good time to point out how faith differences divide a relationship that ought to be "two becoming one." You can cite your own examples of how social life, financial priorities, and ethical philosophies are impacted.

Don't make your husband a villain — bear your own responsibility for any wrong choices you made. But urge your children to consider life in the long term when they enter the romantic scene.

Don't buy the rationale that your teen wants to date an unbeliever so she can win him to the Lord.

WE BLESS OTHER PEOPLE WITH WHAT WE LEARN

The lessons we learn on our mission field will make us effective ambassadors for God with everyone we meet. Giving respect, for example — it's an unmet need for most people in this coarsened, uncaring world.

So will living in the security of God-appointed authority, by cooperating with the authorities who protect you, and by exercising authority over those you protect and provide for (children, employees) with the goal of benefitting them: with clear expectations, adequate instruction, gentle supervision, constant encouragement, and fairness.

So will developing a servant's heart — doing jobs that need to be done instead of speculating about who else should be doing them.

So will developing a quiet spirit, deepening our faith in the Faithful God who keeps us calm in crisis and gracious in relationships.

So will revising our attitudes to please God and to demonstrate that "the will of God is good and acceptable and perfect" (see Romans 12:1, 2).

Then our light will shine from the hilltop as well as in our homes.

BLESSING THE UNIVERSAL CHURCH

Missionary wife, by acting out His commandments, you will exemplify the Virtuous Woman in modern dress to His other daughters.

You can be a champion of godly order in the home, the smallest unit of a godly society. You can inspire others who are "under authority" to pursue righteousness, rather than rights.

You can be a proponent of the re-masculinization of men, by empowering your husband to lead.

Upholding the rightness of wifely submission is likely to be a tough sell, with the fearsome counterfeit of family structure portrayed in foreign cultures, where women are subjugated property, rather than supporting partners in their marriages — or where cults right here in America present caricatures of female submission.

The worldly remedy to heal these distortions is to empower women.

To give the devil his due, perhaps Western women have been reconditioned culturally to strengthen them against events to come — but the godly solution is to empower *the church* to change the hearts of men.

Pray, and pray and pray.

WHAT ONE WOMAN DID

Marjorie, a beloved pillar of a church I used to attend, had been a wheelchair-bound paraplegic since age 15, the year she gave her life to Christ. Her bright smile and genuine interest in people lit up the church when she rolled into her place at a side aisle.

We loved her, and considered her sweet presence among us to be God's gift to us.

But during the seventy years between her new birth and her death, she spent hours in prayer, and more hours in handwritten correspondence with generations of missionaries in foreign countries.

At her death, our pastor received letters from many of her penpals, describing how much they counted on her prayers, how much encouragement they received from her postal friendship, and what a loss they felt. Her life had a worldwide impact.

BLESSING OUR NATION

Do you spend as much time praying for our nation as you do decrying the ways it is falling into ruin?

Prayerlessness is often called the "great sin of the church." Periodically, we hear sermons based on II Chronicles 7:13-14: "If I shut up heaven that there be no rain, or if I command the locusts to devour the land, or if I send pestilence among my people:

"If *my people*, which are called by my name, shall humble themselves, and pray, and seek my face, and turn from their wicked ways: then will I hear from heaven and will forgive their sin, and will heal their land."

This scripture addresses several other sins of the church besides prayerlessness — lack of humbling ourselves before God, neglecting to seek His face, and lack of repentance.

We need to do all four things — just asking for the rain to come, or the locusts and pestilence to go, doesn't meet God's conditions for Him to *heal our land.*

You, missionary wife, are one of His people — and a qualified intercessor. You can take part in this petition for God's deliverance right from your home.

You are already fulfilling the conditions: humbling yourself in the role of submissive servant, seeking the fullness of God's presence in your life, turning from your wicked ways in order to become that chaste, God-fearing woman of I Peter 3.

All you need to add are specific petitions for healing of our country's social ills and for recovery of our power and position in a world that needs moral authority. Pray for protection of our children, protection of biblical marriage, for godly wisdom to guide our leaders.

We, of all people in the church, understand what life would be like if we lose the freedom to worship together. Is the day far away when the American church, like churches in other nations, will have to go underground?

We have already lost many freedoms which I took for granted as a young adult: the freedom to express my faith at work, both verbally and with those knickknacks that husbands don't like; the freedom to have a weekly bible study with other Christians in the company cafeteria during our lunch break.

School prayer used to be part of morning assembly not many years ago; so were Christmas plays, carol-singing in the classroom, community Christmas trees, and "Merry Christmas" greetings by store clerks. While "multiculturalism" is exalted, Christianity is singled out for extinction.

Will it make a difference if you pray for our nation?

Scripture doesn't indicate how many of His people have to participate to turn God's hand, although we have a biblical precedent in Abraham's intercession for Sodom in Genesis 18:23-33. The Lord said He would not destroy Sodom if there were ten righteous people found there.

A better question — will it make a difference if you *don't* pray?

PRAY GLOBALLY, ACT LOCALLY

You can be one of the valuable intercessors who "stand in the gap" not just for our nation, but for this wicked world and its due judgment. Scripture calls for many prayer subjects which rarely make it into the typical Christian's hurry-up prayer time:

- prayer for leaders and authorities, both here and abroad, and *for all men everywhere that we may lead a quiet and peaceable life in all godliness and honesty.*
- in particular, prayer for our enemies — personal and national
- prayer for the Lord of the Harvest to send workers into all the unevangelized fields
- prayer for those workers — their needs, their protection, their success
- prayer for the persecuted, the imprisoned, the oppressed.

This valuable work is something you can do apart from church attendance — while you sit at that aggravatingly slow traffic light on your morning commute, while you fold laundry or empty the dishwasher. And when you take the time for concentrated prayer, your bedside rug or that lowly bathmat can be a power center of invocation.

PRAY 'BROADLY'

When you pray for your own needs, ask God also to meet the same need in other people.

Especially pray for other household missionaries — for their needs, their protection, their strength to persevere, for their success.

Your challenges are the common lot of many women — and your husband's needs are shared by many men.

Consider that, while you are alone in your home, you are far from alone in the business of household ministry.

Pray fervently and effectually for the man you know so intimately. Then add your prayers for your colleagues' husbands: for removal of hindrances to belief, for quickened spiritual interest, for the Lord to send extra workers who will be free to speak the gospel to them, for points of breakthrough.

COUNT YOUR BLESSINGS

There is real power in contentment. It's the antitoxin to bitterness, covetousness, and discouragement.

Keep positive in every thought and every circumstance. God has promised that He is for us, not against us — so get wisdom from examining every trial you go through for its positive potential. And thank Him for it by faith, until you see the hidden treasure.

Here's a suggested inventory for your count:

- Your marriage: you are not alone, you are not settling for a sinful relationship. The man you love has committed himself to you.
- Your husband: By choosing to stay in your spiritually-divided relationship, your husband is confirmed as "God's man for you." He is sanctified — set apart for God's purpose — in your family.
- Your husband's love: The spiritual bond between you and your man is there. He loves you, however little it may be evident.
- Your children: Consider each one separately, and count the ways they enrich your life.
- Your home: This is a work in progress that you and the Lord can turn into your own little patch of Heaven on earth. Count the good times, the happy events, the times of refuge and safety you have experienced within the walls of your dwelling.
- The Lord's abiding presence: He makes Himself at home in your heart — another piece of Heaven on earth. Spend much time rejoicing in the Lord!
- Your ministry: We have a God-appointed assignment, a comfortable mission site, and a harvest field whom we already love.
- Friendships (his, mine and ours): Count the times you knew that you could rely on another person when you needed a listening ear, a helping hand, encouragement. Now count the times when you were privileged to be that ear, hand or encourager.
- Your spiritual life: God has revealed Himself to us in His word and through His Holy Spirit. Count the ways you have learned new facets of God's personality, seen evidence of His love, understood how to walk in His ways. Review your progress in overcoming fears, casting your worries into His lap, realizing His victory over temptation, using His power to tear down a long-standing stronghold.

Look at your treasure trove every day.

BLESSINGS TO COME

That stark verse in 1 Corinthians 7:16 —"For what knowest thou, O wife, *whether* thou shalt save thy husband?" — keeps all our ministry inside the realm of faith. We are not guaranteed that our husbands will believe.

But we do know that our God is a God of reward. He loves our obedience, He loves our endurance and perseverance, He prizes our steady peace (that "quiet spirit") — it is His intention that our joy be made full.

I Timothy 6:17-19 says, "Charge them that are rich in this world, that they be not highminded, not trust in uncertain riches, but in the living God, who giveth us richly all things to enjoy;

"That they do good, that they be rich in good works, ready to distribute, willing to communicate;

"Laying up in store for themselves a good foundation against the time to come, that they may lay hold on eternal life."

Whatever our husbands decide, we can hold onto the confidence that we have been stepping stones for them, not stumbling blocks.

We know that every time we fail — we have, and we will — God will be our Comforter and Redeemer. He will not condemn us. He is likely to use the events we consider to be irreparable to dazzle us with a gracious outcome.

So, we will have both positive and negative stories to tell others as we advance in our faith. We will be "expert witnesses," better and better acquainted with His ways, which are always higher than our ways.

CHURCH COMES TO LOTTIE

Lottie needed more help than her children could provide, so she reluctantly agreed to move to a "retirement village."

A few months later, church came to her.

The pastor of a church located near Lottie's residence offered to bring his Tuesday morning bible study group to the facility, since one of his former participants had moved there. It was open to anyone who wanted to attend.

Lottie asked Harriet to go with her to check it out, and it was just Lottie's cup of tea. The people who came with the pastor were senior citizens, dressed in everyday clothes and sensible shoes, the hymns were old standards that Lottie had known all her life, the bible study well-prepared and interactive.

She attended faithfully until her health required her to move to a higher level of care.

LOTTIE AND HARRIET - EPILOGUE

Lottie passed away just before Thanksgiving two years ago.

The pastor scheduled for her memorial had a medical emergency, so Lottie's elder son stepped in and conducted the service. His remarks followed the biography in Proverbs 31 — the Virtuous Woman, whose children rose up and called her blessed. Two other children added their memories of the home Lottie had made for them.

Lottie and Bud raised six children to responsible adulthood. All are now believers. The two youngest daughters were baptized when they made personal decisions for Christ in their teen years.

AS YOU SUSPECTED

You have guessed by now that I am Harriet — my first name. Other names have been disguised to respect privacy.

This is our story of two spiritually-divided homes — and the gracious, sovereign God who undergirds our efforts and works in His way, in our behalf, despite our mistakes.

As I reflect on my parents' lives, their closest friends were people of faith.

Besides beloved Mrs. See, who figured in both our stories, there were Rey and Via. Dad met Rey when we first moved to New Mexico, and admired Rey's skill as a machinist. He felt Rey was underemployed in the automotive shop where he worked.

Rey had only attended school through eighth grade before he had to go to work to help support his mother. He was grateful for the job he had.

But Dad helped him fill out the papers he needed to apply for a job at a research facility. He was hired, and some of Rey's fine work took flight in the space program. Rey and his wife Via were lifelong friends, and devout people of God.

Then, with the old power wagon long retired, Dad bought a passenger bus and converted it into a motorhome. But he was no longer as strong and nimble as he had been when he built the house trailer for his bride. So he hired a young man named Levi to help him. They became fast friends

When Levi's dad passed away, Levi adopted Dad, visiting him almost every day to check on his welfare. Levi's part of their daily interchange was the natural report of his life as a follower of Christ, which Bud listened to without comment. He couldn't be impolite to someone who treated him with such devotion.

There were Cal and Naomi, a lovely Christian couple, who traveled in caravan with Bud and Lottie on motorhome trips all through the western states and deep into Mexico over a period of many years.

I've no doubt that prayers went up daily for both my parents from friends who loved them with the love of God.

As for me — ?

I've spent far too much time AWOL — away from my mission site, doing good works, but not the *best* ones — not the works only I can do.

Hopefully, I've started to resolve some of the murky advice about how to help a husband toward belief.

And God is putting my allies in place — great Christian people who have entered our lives, not through my church connections, but through friendship with my husband.

I've peacefully withdrawn from the frenetic pace of too much church work, and into the task set before me. I'm finding my Lord's yoke *is* easy, and His lessons are rich and sweet.

EXERCISE 1
GETTING DOWN TO BUSINESS: COUNT YOUR BLESSINGS!

- God has given us revelation of Himself in His word and through His Holy Spirit. All we presently need to know about Him is available to us.
- We have received redemption from our sin nature and cleansing for our personal sins through the blood of Jesus Christ.
- We stand before God in the righteousness of Jesus Christ.
- We have been grafted into the Vine, the life of the Lord Jesus Christ.
- We are blessed with all spiritual blessings in heavenly places in Christ.
- God has given us a comfortable mission field to work in, surrounded by people we love. He has given us everything we need for life and godliness.
- We have instant access to Mission Headquarters through prayer for every situational need.
- We are blessed to be a blessing. Blessing others — especially our husbands and children — is our high calling and purpose.
- We have the resources of a local church for pastoral care, counsel, prayer support, instruction, and participation in baptism and communion.

Add your personal blessings:

-
-
-
-
-
-

Reflect on these truths, and thank God for them often.

EXERCISE 2
ANOTHER SACRIFICE OF THANKSGIVING

Hebrews 13:15-16 says, "...let us offer the sacrifice of praise to God continually, that is, the fruit of our lips giving thanks to his name.

"But to do good and to communicate forget not: for with such sacrifices God is well pleased."

What blessings have you taken for granted? Make a list:

- health
- mobility
- religious freedom
- political freedom
-
-
-
-

Favorite possessions, activities, associates:

-
-
-
-

People who have guided and developed you in your faith. Who led you to Christ? Who prayed for you before you became a believer?

-
-
-
-

Thank God for this record of blessings when you face a disappointment, a dark day, or a time of spiritual coldness.

EXERCISE 3
PRAYER FOR THE NEGLECTED TOPICS - ON BEHALF OF THE UNIVERSAL CHURCH

I Timothy 2:1-4 says, "I exhort therefore, that, first of all, supplications, prayers, intercessions, and giving of thanks, be made for all men;

"For kings, and for all that are in authority: that we may lead a quiet and peaceable life in all godliness and honesty.

"For this is good and acceptable in the sight of God our Saviour;

Who will have all men to be saved, and to come unto the knowledge of the truth."

- pray for all mankind
- pray for leaders of the nations of the world
- pray for America's national leaders
- pray for your state's leaders, county and city leaders
- pray for law enforcement personnel and judges
- pray for church leaders throughout the world
- pray for business or educational leaders in your life

Matthew 5:44 says, "...Love your enemies, bless them that curse you, do good to them that hate you, and pray for them which despitefully use you, and persecute you."

- pray for personal enemies: people from whom you are estranged or with whom you have a painful history. Pray for the power to forgive, and for resolution, healing and restoration of love and good will.

- pray for ideological enemies: people whose religious, philosophical or political stances stir ugly feelings in you. Disregard the issues that separate you, and ask God to open your heart to identify and pray for their needs.

- pray for "enemies of the people" - ask that the light of God's love will penetrate dark hearts, and that He will restrain their power to do evil
  - for foreign leaders who desire our country's downfall
  - for agents of foreign powers at work inside our borders

- for gangs and members of organized crime
- for individuals plotting random violence

⁕ pray for captives of our enemies; for the safety of Christians who live in enemy nations and for individuals in those countries who long for peace and freedom.

EXERCISE 4
EQUIP YOUR CHILDREN WITH SKILLS FOR A SUCCESSFUL LIFE

What you can teach apart from "religious instruction"
Issues of stewardship:

- Health management:
  - why we need good nutrition
  - why we need adequate rest and sleep
  - why we need to exercise

- Money management:
  - how to budget money earned or given as allowance
  - how to economize where they have some control
  - the wisdom of saving
  - the joy of giving
  - distinguishing between "price" and "value"

- Time management:
  - how to establish priorities
  - the virtue of being prompt

Relational skills:

- Problem-solving:
  - the importance of courtesies
  - taking responsibility: truthfulness, admitting wrongs, meeting needs
  - making amends: apology and restitution
  - understanding grace and forgiveness
  - how to negotiate a conflict
  - how to overlook an offense
  - how to look at another person's viewpoint

- Work ethic
  - the connection between work and money
  - the importance of following instructions
  - the structure of authority
  - work's contribution to the general good
  - the joy of work well done

EXERCISE 5
LOOK ON THE FIELD: SHARING HIS INTERESTS

From Chapter 6, Exercise 4, list your husband's most fervent interests:

Rank them in order of their importance to him:

Would you say any of his interests are as inportant to him as is your interest in church activities?

How much support do you give him for his pet interests? Do you encourage him to share them with you, or do you compartmentalize your lives so that "he does his thing and you do your (church) thing"?

Has compartmentalization of interests caused any conflict or caused a loss of communication between you?

How can you, as far as it lies within your power, rebuild a sharing of his interests into your marriage?

How might Jesus' Golden Rule ("Therefore all things whatsoever ye would that men should do to you, do ye even so to them...") apply in opening a route to share your interests with your husband?

CHAPTER 10

Equipping Household Missionaries

The Neglected Workers

LOOK FOR THE 'LOTTIES' IN YOUR CHURCH

One side effect of our persistent affliction — self-pity — is the feeling that we're the only ones in our pitiful situation.

But a thoughtful study of your church congregation will give you an idea of how pervasive spiritually-unequal marriages are. Women outnumber men in almost every church. While the majority may be single, divorced, or widowed, many will have husbands who choose to spend their Sundays elsewhere.

So — are you alert to greet a "Lottie" who visits your church? Do you say "hello," exchange names, invite her to sit beside you?

How about introducing her to another friend or to a church leader as well?

Don't pry for information, but make her feel like she has come to a place that welcomes her as a sister in Christ.

When a sister household missionary is absent from service, give her a call to tell her you missed her. Read the bulletin announcements to her.

Pick up a tape of the sermon for her, if you think it was one she shouldn't miss.

WHO WILL GO FOR US?

If your church does not offer a training class or a support group for unequally-yoked wives, see what you can do to start one.

Isaiah 6:8 says, "Also I heard the voice of the Lord, saying, Whom shall I send, and who will go for us? Then said I, Here am I; send me."

Begin with prayer for guidance. Then make an appointment to talk to your pastor.

Prepare for your meeting by developing a good proposal. Pastors resist "upward delegation" — dumping a need at his doorstep with the expectation that he will take on work you assign.

So go with an appealing approach:

1. Express the need.
2. Show him this book and offer to leave it with him to review.
3. Suggest how the class could be designed and publicized.
4. End with the "here am I" offer to lead the group.

THE NEED

Briefly tell him your personal struggle of trying to follow Christ apart from your husband — how the conflicting demands of churchlife and homelife leave you feeling unsatisfied on both fronts.

Tell him your desire: for wives to be equipped with biblical strategies for this distinctive mission field: to "win their husbands without a word."

Point out that missionaries to foreign fields and to domestic target groups are equipped for ministry — and that household missionaries need similar preparation.

Inquire if he knows how many women in the congregation are married to men whose faith is lukewarm or absent. Tell him of women you know who would be potential participants in an equipping class.

One heads-up: be prepared for some surprises. Some women are so used to their divided state that it is a "comfort zone" they may be reluctant to disturb. Give God time to prepare them for a future class.

THIS BOOK

Offer to let your pastor examine this book, which is designed with a two-fold purpose: an individual woman can use it as her handbook, expanding the rationale and detail of the usual advice to "pray, let your light shine, and leave him in God's hands."

It offers assessment exercises for her to personalize its principles: to gain understanding of her husband's resistance, to remove the stumbling blocks she herself may have placed in the way of his belief, and to pray effectually for him.

It is also amenable for use as a small-group meeting guide, with bible study questions suitable for discussion. Brainstorming topics are suggested to strengthen relationship with a husband who often draws away from a wife who has become "religious" when he is not. The input of other wives can be very helpful.

PROPOSE A FORMAT

Unequally-yoked women are reluctant to add one more meeting to their schedules when it is a challenge just to get to worship service.

With that in mind, the most workable format would probably be a 6- to 9-week Sunday school elective class, limited to 12 women (eight is ideal, for maximum discussion participation).

The meeting time would be convenient for students who would find it harder to schedule a weekday or evening meeting. If they are regular attendees at worship service, the Sunday school slot would require the least additional time commitment from them.

And, a Sunday school hour has its own built-in end point. Discussion groups without a mandatory cut-off time can involve participants (and leaders) in overly long sessions.

Having a limited time window helps keep everyone focussed on the purpose at hand.

I strongly recommend that you offer a pilot program as a Sunday school class. If there is demand, offer a repeat class, home bible studies, or one-on-one mentoring by women who have completed the class.

HOW TO PUBLICIZE THE TRAINING

The church bulletin or newsletter is a good place to announce the new ministry, and to ask for advance signups so you can order books for participants and can plan classroom layout.

A sign-up form should ask for:

Name:
Telephone number:
email address:
Best time/method to contact:
Level of bible knowledge (beginner, intermediate, advanced)

If you get more than 12 enrollees, decide how to accommodate them. If you are the only potential leader, the best option would be to schedule successive groups.

If you are willing and able, you can add a second session to your commitment — or a successive class could be taught by a woman who has completed your pilot class.

Use the level of bible knowledge as a criterion if you need to divide the enrollees into more than one group.

WHAT IF PASTOR WOULD RATHER TEACH THE CLASS HIMSELF?

Celebrate and enroll in it! If he deputizes you to lead the group, read on:

WHY LIMIT CLASS SIZE?

My vision in writing the book was for it to facilitate conversation, where exercises could be discussed and encouragement shared among a few people who would get to know each other over the course of the meetings.

This requires preparation by the students. They read a chapter ahead of time and complete selected exercises for each class. The leader guides discussion.

The small group setting can serve many needs — a place for study, meaningful fellowship and prayer support.

My favorite arrangement is to seat women around a table, with room for their workbooks and bibles. Aim for active involvement from each member by calling on them to read the answers from their homework: portray your gathering as a "missions convention" where you are supporting each other in a specific task — not a grievance group.

ENLIST A CLASSROOM ASSISTANT

The Lord Jesus Christ had a good idea when He sent His disciples out two by two.

An assistant can help you keep track of time so you can dismiss the class without making people late for worship service. She can help keep discussion on track by making "positive redirection" when a participant dominates a discussion or goes too far down a rabbit trail. She can collect prayer petitions at the beginning of class and do "other duties as assigned."

THE ISSUE OF DOMESTIC ABUSE

The possibility that one — or more! — of your participants will be suffering spousal abuse is an incredibly prevalent reality.

Discuss this with your pastor before you begin so you will have guidelines and an action plan for a time when the problem may arise.

Your pastor is best qualified to intervene when a situation comes to your attention.

Be very careful what advice you dispense.

Do not become personally involved in sheltering a woman. This is a dangerous dynamic which could put your family at risk.

Do not make the woman feel like she is to blame — nor that she is in a hopeless situation.

Do encourage her to take protective steps for herself and her children.

Do pray for her diligently.

OTHER CAUTIONS

Women hunger for fellowship, and our situation certainly brings up issues that we'd like to vent to someone who will understand.

However...

It is so important that we remain loyal, positive, and focussed that I do not favor providing open opportunity to discuss "the problem," which leads to complaining and oneupmanship in telling about husbands' faults.

The mission should be to encourage, remind of God's instructions, pray strategically, and love one another.

You will find a commitment list at the back of this chapter, which I recommend reading at the beginning of every class session. Remind the class of those commitments when a member starts to veer off course.

A one-hour meeting will go by very quickly. Start your meetings on time to honor those who are prompt.

If you don't have a teacher's assistant to help you keep track of time, appoint a class member to alert you when it's time to wrap up discussion and go to closing prayer — five to ten minutes before the end of class.

The small group is a perfect place to pray for one another, but it can also be a place where discipline falls apart. Ask for prayer requests to be written out on 3 x 5 cards, and ask that they pertain to the person writing the request and for her immediate household — not for neighbors, friends, job situations, world affairs.

There are other places to seek prayer support for broader needs — use your time at the "missions conference" to pray for missions business.

HANDLING DISTRACTIONS IN CLASS

You have been authorized to provide teaching you have prepared. Don't lend your audience to someone who has an axe to grind or a testimony that exalts herself rather than the Lord, or who simply feels she can do a better job than you are doing. (Even if it's true, she needs to schedule her own meeting!)

And it is your responsibility to protect the time of women for whom church activity is limited and precious.

Bathe your meetings in prayer before you start. If you can recruit a group of women to pray for you *while* you are meeting, ask them to pray for protection against intrusion, confusion, and discord.

Another safeguard is to train your teaching assistant to make "positive interruptions" to help you regain control of your leadership. (Positive interruptions are questions like, "Could we get back to your last comment?" which gives you the opportunity to say, "Yes, let's do that. " And to the interruptor: "Thank you for your input, but we need to finish talking about today's subject.")

THE IMPORTANCE OF PASTORAL COVERING

Because this book encourages women to examine their level of church attendance, it can be misunderstood or misrepresented as a call for women to abandon the church.

Please work *with* your pastor — ask him to cover your meeting with his prayers, invite him to drop in at any time, and report to him regularly as to how things are going.

FOLLOW-UP MINISTRY

If your class wants to continue meeting after they have finished going through the book, perhaps your pastor would help you find a new subject to study together: for example, a book on prayer, on women of the bible, on discipleship, or the Book of Proverbs.

Another plan is to train them to teach the material they have just completed, and bless your pastor with a cadre of women who can mentor wives who are unable to fit into a class schedule, or newly-converted wives who may need basic discipleship.

SUGGESTED CLASS OUTLINE USING A 9-LESSON FORMAT

Tailor the outline to suit your schedule, omitting or combining lessons to shorten the class to a 6-week program. Please write a lesson plan for each meeting to keep discussion focussed and to stay within the allotted time.

SESSION 1

Introductory Meeting

- Preparatory homework: read Chapter 1, "The Dismal Multiplication of Neglect."
- Start class by praying the Prayer for Missionary Wives (Chapter 10, Exercise 1)
- Read Commitment to Rules for Household Missionaries Class together.
- Ask each class member to state her name and to tell her two love stories: how she met and fell in love with her husband, and how she came to faith in the Lord Jesus Christ. Ask your timekeeper to limit each speaker to about three minutes.
- Closing prayer emphasis: forgiveness — of oneself, of the church, of husbands

SESSION 2

The missionary model

- Advance reading: chapter 2, "Neglected Jerusalem"
- Ask a class member to read Psalm 51 as opening prayer
- Ask each member to read the mission statement she has written. Encourage them to refine what they have written as they gain ideas from other women.
- Discuss answers to the bible studies in Exercises 3 and 4 at the end of Chapter 2
- Prayer for written petitions, and closing prayer: Ask God to help each woman develop a "missionary's heart" for her husband, desiring his highest good in God's Kingdom

SESSION 3

Whose you are, where you are

- Advance reading: Chapter 3, "The Neglected Houseguest"

- Ask a class member to read Ephesians 3:14-21 as an opening prayer.
- Discuss answers to the bible study in Exercise 4 at the end of Chapter 3
- Prayer for written petitions, and closing prayer: Ask Jesus to forgive every hindrance to His full abiding in our hearts, and to cleanse us from all unrighteousness.

SESSION 4

The foundation of respect

- Advance reading: Chapter 4, "The Neglected Attitude"
- Ask a class member to read the Prayer for Missionary Wives to begin
- Discuss the issues in Exercises 1-4 at the end of Chapter 4, and if time permits, discuss answers to the bible study in Exercise 5
- Written petitions and closing prayer: pray for the establishment and growth of respect in each marriage

SESSION 5

Setting priorities

Note: INVITE YOUR PASTOR TO ATTEND THIS SESSION!

- Advance reading: Chapter 5, "What *should* you neglect?"
- Ask the pastor to say an opening prayer
- Discuss Exercises 1, 2 and 3, and brainstorm Exercise 4 at the end of Chapter 5 - assure the pastor his input is very welcome in the discussion
- Written petitions and prayer for guidance in setting priorities.
- Thank pastor for his attendance and support

SESSION 6

The dreaded "s" words - submission, sacrifice, suffering

- Advance reading: Chapter 6, "The Neglected Dynamics"
- Open by saying the Lord's Prayer in unison
- Discuss the studies in Exercises 1 and 2 at the back of the chapter
- Written petitions and closing prayer: prayer for deeper identification with the Lord in submission, sacrifice and suffering

SESSION 7

Servanthood

- Advance reading: Chapter 7, "The Neglected Demonstration"
- Before class, turn the chairs with their backs to the table. Invite those

who are willing and able to kneel at their chairs while you read Philippians 2:1-16 as a prayer

- Discuss the answers to the bible studies in Exercises 2 and 5 at the end of the chapter
- Written petitions and closing prayer: pray for each woman to develop a servant's heart

SESSION 8

Communication

- Advance reading: Chapter 8, "The Neglected Art"
- Ask each woman to present the testimony she prepared for Exercise 2 at the end of Chapter 8; discuss answers to questions in Exercise 6
- Optional creative project: build a house from a large sheet of poster board which you have cut in the form of a cross, with the four extensions the same size as the center square. Label the center square: Foundation: respect

Label each of the other four squares (on the back sides, so the labels will appear when the walls are raised): Cooperation, Encouragement, Loyalty and Confidence.

Fold the sides up to form an open box and tape them in place. Cover it with a flat piece of poster board 2-3" wider than the open side of the box. Label it: Husband's Protection. Cut a second board as wide as the husband's roof and 12" longer. Label it: the Lord's Protection. Fold it in half to form a peaked room, and set it over the flat roof.

- Pray for written petitions.
- Going around the table in sequence, ask participants to read one of the scriptures in Exercise 4 as a prayer for husbands.

SESSION 9

Blessed to Bless

- Advance reading: Chapter 9, "The Neglected Distribution"
- Before class, turn chairs with their backs to the table. Invite those who are willing and able to kneel at their chairs while you read Psalm 95:1-6 as a prayer. Invite the class to add sentence prayers of thanksgiving for specific blessings before you say "Amen."
- Turn to Exercise 3 at the back of Chapter 9, and ask class members to pray for the neglected topics (omitting prayer for personal enemies).
- End with the Prayer for Missionary Wives.

EXERCISE 1
PRAYER FOR MISSIONARY WIVES

Dearest Father,

Thank You for the deep assurance that with You all things are possible.

I thank You for my husband and for my Lord Jesus Christ — the two loves of my life.

I thank You for the wisdom of Your Word, and for the teaching of the Holy Spirit as I study Your ways.

Father, I make special petition for the desire of my heart, that my husband may come to believe in and love my Savior as I do. I pray for your guidance in all I do, to make me a stepping stone, not a stumbling block, to his faith in Jesus Christ.

I ask your protection for myself and for all missionary wives

- for avoidance of adultery in any form: physical, spiritual or emotional
- for victory over self-pity and self-righteousness
- for freedom from self-condemnation.

Father, protect us from judging our men against Christians standards which they can't possibly keep, apart from Your presence in their lives.

Protect us from feeling they are fair game for criticism to other women — and from blindness to our disloyalty.

Keep us ever grateful for their contributions to our lives, and for the marital bond which keeps us together. May we honor that bond as You do.

Amen

EXERCISE 2
COMMITMENT TO RULES FOR HOUSEHOLD MISSIONARY CLASS

1. I will not dishonor my husband by revealing any information that he would not want broadcast. (Tell others only the things about him that you would be willing for him to share about you.)

2. I will keep confidential any information other women reveal which could hurt their spouses or other people not present.

3. I will not raise argumentative questions in class, but will request a private meeting with the leader or a designated counselor to discuss objections, or to ask questions that do not pertain to the entire group.

4. Recognizing that our time is valuable, I will do my best to arrive promptly to each class.

5. I will write out my prayer requests ahead of class time on a 3 x 5" card. Our group will pray in agreement for requests pertaining to class participants and their immediate families. Again, I will use discretion in expressing needs that could embarrass others.

EXERCISE 3
ON THE CONTRARY: THE DISTINCTIVES OF OUR PARTICULAR MISSION FIELD

Principle One:
Not "the ends of the earth," but "beginning at Jerusalem"
Our homes are worthy and important places to serve Christ

Principle Two:
Not "go and tell" but "stay and show"
We are missionaries with an inverted commission

Principle Three:
Not "a problem to fix" but "a man to love as the Lord loves him"
Respect: the foundation of ministry to him

Principle Four:
Not "ambassadors of the church" but "ambassadors of Christ"
Prioritizing Mary (spiritual) and Martha (practical) time

Principle Five:
Not "called to be served" but "chosen to serve"
Service: the "show" in "show, don't tell"

Principle Six:
Not "in words" but "in demonstration of the spirit and power"
The power of submission, sacrifice and suffering to develop Christlike virtue